Making A World Of Difference...

One Life At A Time

▶ ▶ ▶ ▶ ▶

▶ **World Vision.** The vision continues. And it *will* continue as long as there's a need...as long as children are hurting...as long as we serve a purpose in our Lord's name.

But in order for our vision to continue, we need you. You are the life link to the children we serve. Through Childcare Sponsorship, you ensure that a child has the basic necessities of life...food, clothing, health care, education.

▶ **The child's community also benefits.** Through things like clean water, schools, medical clinics, agricultural improvements, and vocational training, the dream of a better future can be shared by all.

Twenty dollars a month. That's all it takes. About 65 cents a day helps fill a priceless life with dignity and hope.

▶ **Become a part of the vision.** Become a World Vision Childcare Sponsor.

So that a child may have many tomorrows.

▸ ▸

I want to become part of the vision.

Please send me information and a photograph today of a child who needs my help. I prefer a ☐ girl ☐ boy from ☐ Africa ☐ Asia ☐ South America ☐ Where the need is greatest.

☐ Enclosed is my first monthly payment of $20.

☐ I can't sponsor a child right now but would like to contribute $ _____ .
(1700)

World Vision Childcare Sponsorship, Pasadena, California 91131

Name _____

Address _____

City/State/Zip _____

AX0000   Your sponsorship payments are tax deductible.

Mozambique—photo by David Ward

Making a World of Difference

Difference

One Life at a Time

Robert A. Seiple

PRESIDENT OF WORLD VISION

WORD PUBLISHING

Dallas · London · Vancouver · Melbourne

ONE LIFE AT A TIME

Copyright © 1990 by World Vision

All rights reserved. No portion of this book, text or pictures, may be used without the written permission of the publisher, except for brief quotations in critical reviews or articles.

All Scripture quotations are from the King James Version.

Library of Congress Cataloging-in-Publication Data

Seiple, Robert A., 1942–
  One life at a time / by Robert A. Seiple.
    p.   cm.
  ISBN 0-8499-0828-0 : $12.99 — ISBN 0-8499-3268-8 (pbk.) : $8.99
  1. World Vision International.   I. Title.
BV2360.W885S45   1990
267'.13—dc20   90-42535
                                                                   CIP

Printed in the United States of America

0 1 2 3 4 9 RRD 10 9 8 7 6 5 4 3 2 1

To *Sintayehus,* whom I promised not to forget.

To those whose stories fill these pages:

Whose dignity in the face of poverty
spoke of their eternal value,
Whose hope in the face of disaster
caused us all to continue our labors,
Whose love to their neighbor
convicted all our hearts.

To the names we have yet to learn,
The faces we have yet to see,
The hearts we have yet to touch.

◆ ◆ ◆

Acknowledgments

My grateful thanks to the following, without whom this book would not have taken shape:

- James and Lyric Murphy, for their vision and dedication to the message of this book, and for their research, organization and editing of story material.

- Jerry Sweers, for keeping these stories alive and moving us through a critical phase in producing this book.

- The original storytellers, eyewitnesses and story resource people, including:

Judy Blain	Larry Ward
Graeme Irvine	David Ward
Pam Kerr	Kenny Waters
W. Stanley Mooneyham	Barbara Weisbrod
Bob Pierce	Ron Wilson
David Ritchie	

- Laurel Hone and Word Publishing, for their initiative and support in seeing this message brought to completion.

Contents

◆ ◆ ◆

Preface

This book was originally conceived as a commemorative of World Vision's 40th anniversary.

As it began to take shape, however, it refused to be forced into the mold of an organizational history. Rather, the message upon which the organization was founded kept surfacing as the most important—indeed the only—reason to write the book. I intended this book to be about those who give and those who receive, but I discovered that in many situations, the roles were reversed. So often I received more than I gave.

You will not read about history, therefore. To compile an exhaustive—or even remotely complete—history of World Vision would take many volumes. What you will read about are selected personal encounters that illustrate and exemplify the message of hope, reconciliation and transformation that is the foundation for all that we do.

In the final analysis, the events themselves are not as important as the people who participated in them. It is not the organization that has value, but the human beings whose dedication, sacrifice and service give it life.

And, although the people are served within the context of sometimes large, complex, multi-national projects and programs, we must never lose sight that the structure is only to facilitate changing lives, one life at a time.

This is a very personal book—written about individual events that have taken place over the last 40 years. It is not meant to highlight our most important achievements, nor to act as a catalog of the most significant events that have shaped our organization during that time. Instead, it simply tells the stories that have touched me personally. Stories which have changed my life as Christ has ministered to me as president of an organization I firmly believe He has empowered and directed over these last four decades.

I pray that they challenge you personally as well.

Robert A. Seiple
June 1990

◆ ◆ ◆

Introduction

I have a secret to share with you.

The answers to some of the big problems of our world today—poverty, hunger, disease—are little ones. They are little solutions that, when added up, have an enormous impact. Forty years of ministry at World Vision have been built on the simple little acts of compassion that make a world of difference in one person's life. Experience has shown that ordinary people—people just like you and me—can have an extraordinary impact on a child's life. We see those changes one life at a time, but the cumulative effect can transform a community, a country, and eventually, even the whole world.

The danger in trying to grapple with the complex issues of our world today is that we depersonalize them. "Poverty" is just too big. If I have learned anything in my years here at World Vision, I have learned that poverty has a face.

And hunger has a name.

It is not a generic face or name, but one belonging to one individual—one mother's child. One father's precious first-born. Or a helpless mother whose eyes are filled with anxiety and frustration at her inability to care for her infant properly.

Some of what you'll read I have experienced myself. Some has been passed down a generation. Original story-tellers include both World Vision staff and those touched by our projects. But, like all good stories, they reflect the deep realities and values which motivate us as human beings and as Christians.

Working at World Vision is a personal journey of growth, of challenge, of confronting the painful conditions in the Developing World. But more than anything, it has been a time of renewing the hope that, together, we can make a difference in the lives of others—whether they're halfway around the world, or right down the street.

These are stories of everyday people facing overwhelming circumstances—true accounts of how persons like you and me act when they meet poverty face to face . . . or what they find in the deepest recesses of their hearts when they learn the name of hunger. If you will allow your heart the room to respond—you will see your own compassion mirrored in their actions.

The strength, vision and hope exhibited by those you'll read about can revive a tired heart, rekindle a flagging faith, stir anew compassion for our neighbor. It is a true picture—these are the lessons all of us know in our spirit. We need only to practice these precepts in our daily lives.

I have learned that hope is rekindled one heart at a time.

In the spring of 1989, I traveled to a refugee camp in the Sudan, the site of a bitter and vicious civil war. Upon landing on a small dirt runway, I had the feeling that something had gone horribly wrong. For the children, life had somehow been divided in two—half were orphaned, half carried the visible scars of malnourishment. Mortality for children was running at even greater than half. The sanctity of human life was taking second seat to military tactics, with the children caught in the crossfire. Innocent children were being sacrificed to human pride. And this—in a relatively secure part of the country. Death hung heavy in the air. I couldn't even imagine what it must be like closer to the fighting . . . .

When we actually arrived at the camp, many of the people were naked. Their only clothing was made of burlap sacks. The only water was rain water. Fortunately, it had rained two days before our arrival. The bad news was that the water was absolutely filthy. It was mud brown in color and full of floating debris.

I met a 12-year-old boy who had been separated from his parents. He was sick—anemic, undernourished. Under a scorching noonday sun, he sat crumpled in the dust, too weak and listless to move. He was too sick to give us his name. A smile had not crossed that young face in a long time.

Everything about him spoke of a broken spirit. If he somehow managed to survive, the scars of losing parents, home, land and stable future would impact him for the rest of his life.

I found it hard to compare him to my own 12-year-old son. Just at the age when we expect a time of self-discovery, expanding horizons and newly forming aspirations for the future, this tragic young lad had lost all hope. His life had been stolen from him. He had given up. I have learned that hope is rekindled one heart at a time.

I have learned that there are no limits to love.

Sitting across a small wooden table in Da Nang, Vietnam, I listened to a father tenderly tell the story of the 15-year-old child beside him.

It was beautiful to watch the father talk. His eyes said it all. So much compassion, so much love. And the child needed all of both. He was blind and mentally retarded.

The relationship between the man and the boy was a miracle in itself. In the last turbulent days of the war, the man's wife had been involved in a brief affair with another man. She had become pregnant. By the time the child was born, her remorse was so great that she attempted to kill her child.

She nearly succeeded. Leaving the house, she went into a remote area, dug a shallow grave and buried the child alive. But her husband was already looking for her, and he found her bending over the fresh mound of dirt. Working feverishly, he dug the infant out, but not before the lack of oxygen had rendered the child permanently blind and severely retarded.

The father took the distraught wife and broken child home. He gave the boy a name—his name—Tran Dinh Loi. He loved him as his own, and his love for his wife transcended the enormity of her sin.

In the intervening years, a voice of rare and wonderful beauty developed in the young lad. He used it now to sing Vietnamese love songs for us. He sang softly with a smile that spread across his face, his head moving from side to side—a Vietnamese Stevie Wonder. When he sang, we felt the love and compassion of the adoptive father flowing from this young life.

A scandalous birth had emerged out of the brokenness of a fallen world. Sin was buried in a grave that ultimately could not contain the body. That body was rescued by a father whose love was greater than his personal pain. The unfaithful wife was completely forgiven. Her sins were remembered no more.

We sat around a small wooden table in a poor household and listened to a child's love songs. Oh, the richness of love, the incomprehensibility of forgiveness! I have learned that there are no limits to love.

I have learned that we share a common pain.

Our neighbor is simply the one who needs us—regardless of where he/she may be. In Jesus' time, that meant the Samaritan—halfbreed, outcast, stranger—reaching out to the Hebrew. One element of the parable of the Good Samaritan that we often miss and which makes it more powerful is that it is the story of a "have not" reaching out to a "have." One person's compassion reaching out in the midst of another person's adversity. No celebration, no fanfare, just a quiet, tangible expression of love. Yet the lessons contained in that single act have changed lives for 20 centuries.

The parable does not tell of the casual philanthropy of a wealthy businessman, but the sacrificial giving of a poor person—or at the very most, an average worker like you and me—who knew he could make a difference personally.

And that's been the strength of World Vision—providing a channel for individuals to respond to that deep witness in their own spirits, knowing that their compassion can reach into the pain of another and reduce it. In a very real sense, we do this by sharing a common pain.

Yes, it hurts to be hungry. It hurts to lose a child to a disease when a fifty-cent inoculation could have saved him or her. Our minds reel at the thought of such a tragedy—and our hearts feel the pain enough to want to help relieve it.

When I first traveled overseas, I braced myself to witness the suffering of nations—buttressed my internal defenses against the onslaught of a thousand starving refugees all clamoring for food. I felt it necessary in order to be able to function.

God had other plans. I was ready to confront the struggle of thousands, but completely unprepared for the first dying child I held in my arms. This was no statistic.

This was a little girl whose life was draining out of her even as I watched her chest heave with the exertion of drawing another breath. It did not matter that we had met only moments before—we were linked in a bond that reached to the very core of my being.

In that moment, I caught a glimpse of the awesome, underlying agony of God when even the least of His children perish. To refrain from parting the very heavens and reaching into that dusty tent was possible, I believe, only because there is coming a day when every sleeping child shall rise and every grave will empty in response to a mighty "Come forth!" that shall echo in hearts for all eternity.

That day, I saw a little of what it means to see as Christ sees. For He sees not as we do—the dirty, smudgefaced little skin-covered skeleton whose tragic misfortune it was to be born in the midst of a famine or war. Rather, He sees the brightly burning candle of God's own creation asking only for a little more time to shine on this earth.

Yet I know that He endured anguish beyond my comprehension in order to relight the candle of His presence in my spirit—and in hers.

It is in sharing that common pain that I find strength—strength to reach out to another child who I know will break my heart again. Strength to work today for the hope of tomorrow. Strength to give to others simply because I receive strength from Him, the source of all power and might and glory.

I have learned that we share a common pain.

Both Moses and Jesus began their lives as refugees. They wandered in uncertain times before unpredictable rulers and in the midst of people whose motivations were a complex web of desire, need and history. The story of Christianity is the story of faith becoming reality when everything the eye can see is arrayed against it. It is the story of miracles.

So come along with me to witness some miracles. Not the lightning bolt from on high, but the miracles of changed hearts, transformed lives and renewed minds.

I pray you find lessons for yourself among these pages. I trust that, wherever you are in your journey of faith, these stories will inspire, strengthen and encourage you as well.

Kapuchea—Photo by Eric Mooneyham

Part I

◆ ◆ ◆ ◆ ◆ ◆ ◆ ◆ ◆ ◆ ◆ ◆

Let Us Remember
Their Names

Mozambique (Jacinto)—photo by David Ward

◆ ◆ ◆

Sintayehus of Ethiopia

I met an old woman at a feeding station in Ajibar, Ethiopia. It was in the fall of 1987—at the height of the second great Ethiopian famine of the 1980s. She was dressed in rags. Her face was wrinkled, weathered, and her teeth were crooked and broken. Although she was surrounded by thousands of other hungry people, as I learned the severity of her plight, her very presence tugged at the sleeve of my conscience. She had lost so much. . . .

When the first famine hit in 1984, she was married and had eight wonderful children. She was full of hope and happiness, supported by the love of those around her. But famine is an unrelenting thief.

One by one, it stole the life from seven of her children. She watched helplessly as they slowly weakened. Their struggle to live gradually became less intense as the bitter lethargy of starvation invaded their bodies, their hearts and—finally in death—their spirits.

The tears flowed freely as she recounted their names. Starvation has been described as death by inches. Seven children wasting away is a lot of inches. . . .

The world had watched Ethiopia's national trauma from a distance, but here before me was the personal tragedy that had been repeated a million times. Suddenly the numbers were replaced by a sea of individual faces, each one with a private story of loss that set him or her apart.

People don't suffer as a group, they suffer intimately, personally and, ultimately, alone. And despite our tendency to do so, multiplying the suffering on a national scale does not diminish it for the individual. Yes, the old woman had witnessed many of her neighbors lose children as well. But they were still *her* children who were now gone. The babe that suckled your own breast will never be just another face in a crowd.

Just months before the famine finally broke and food was once again available, her husband died in the same camp in which she now stood.

And now the famine had returned. Only this time, the people were much more vulnerable. The cattle were gone, as were the sheep, the chickens, the rest of the livestock. But more devastating—so were many of their families.

This woman's tears, it was clear, were not only for the pain of the past, but for the fear of the future. She was old, she was hungry—and she was alone.

Her monthly ration of food had just been stolen. She had set it down to get some help carrying it back to her village, and when she returned, it was gone. Her voucher said she was entitled to nothing more for another month. What little hope she had for survival had just been snatched away.

The morning we learned her story, my wife, Margaret Ann, cut through the bureaucracy and got the woman a new supply of food. Before she left, I asked her what else I could do. Her answer still echoes in my mind, "Please don't let the people of the world forget Ethiopia."

I was amazed that in that woman's heart—far from the media and most of civilization—grew a sobering intuition as strong as the hunger gnawing in her stomach: this time, both the resources and the compassion of the world might fail.

I came home determined that the world would not forget, and told many of my colleagues her story. "Bob, that was a powerful story," one of them said, "but you never told us her name."

That remark, offered almost casually, shook me deeply. You see, I didn't remember.

Was I there just to get a story to put together a heart-tugging financial appeal? Was she a real person, or just a vehicle to arouse emotion somewhere on the other side of the world? Did I unwittingly depersonalize her, take away the dignity she has as a child of God?

It is so hard, sometimes, to remember that even the largest crowds are made up of individuals with their own personal dreams, hopes, fears, hurts and memories—especially when the unrelenting hand of famine or disaster has reduced them all to rags and skeletons.

The morning after we met the woman, other World Vision staff and I watched the people appearing on the horizon at dawn on their way to the feeding station. Their numbers made them but dots on the landscape. They were just faraway people in a faraway place with faraway needs.

But they are God's children, our neighbors. And they have names.

The woman's name was Sintayehus.

Fifty-six years old, she looked ancient and was considered so in a country where the average life expectancy is only 41. She lost her husband, four sons and three daughters to hunger and disease.

I promised her we would not forget Ethiopia, and I promised myself I would not forget Sintayehus because of the oppressed and forgotten people she represents.

There *is* hope. It will take time and perseverance on both their part and ours—a mutual effort celebrating the worth and promise of all humankind. So as we work to restore their hope, let us do everything possible to preserve their dignity.

Let us remember their names.

A Bruised Reed, a Broken Flower, a Bright Hope

I watched the boy sleeping quietly under his hospital sheet. Where his left leg should have been, the sheet lay smoothly on the bed. His right leg ended at the knee. The bandages at the end of his right arm still needed to be changed regularly because of the fluids seeping through the pulpy mass of tissue that was all that remained of his hand.

The boy had stepped on a land mine—another innocent victim of the vicious civil war in Mozambique.

His parents had carried his shattered body to the hospital, despairing of his survival. They said his name was "Chicaiba Maopa," which means "receiver of bad luck." Even if he lived, they said there was no way they could have cared for him. So they would not be back. There were too many maimed or crippled children already. Live or die, in the harsh world of war, they were saying good-bye to him.

That had been four months ago. When the boy regained consciousness for the first time, the nurse called him Chicaiba. He protested, "That's not my name! I'm Jacinto."

Jacinto means hyacinth, a beautiful flower, one whose life is promised to blossom. Apparently the last thing his parents did when they dropped him off was change his name. The name given in great hope and with the promise for a new life that would grow and bloom like a beautiful flower had been taken away.

In its place, the flower had been cursed.

And so I found myself standing by the bedside of this 12-year-old boy wondering, *what's in a name?* Is it just a convenient attachment to avoid confusion? Then perhaps a number would do as well. But in many cultures, a person's name is carefully chosen to reflect his or her character, the parents' hopes, dreams and aspirations for the young child's future.

God considers names so important that it was one of the first things the angel told Mary about her Son. Adam was given the task of naming all of creation. That act signified his uniqueness. We are told that the Savior has our name engraved on the palms of His hand. And someday the ultimate sign of our new nature will be a new name given to us by God.

It's an important event when names are given. Even more significant when names are changed.

In ancient Jewish tradition, a 12-year-old boy would be completing his temple schooling and preparing to assume the name of his father. This was a major milestone, signifying the transition into manhood and guaranteeing a part of his father's inheritance.

In our culture, the twelfth year signifies the end of childhood as well. At that age children are about to enter the period that strikes fear into every parent's heart. They are about to become teenagers. As neither a child nor an adult, these turbulent years are marked by the struggle to learn self identity, to learn who they will be in the adult world. Often it is a time when the diminutive names, like Bobby, are dropped once and for all. Bobby is gone along with the little boy. Bob, the man, now endeavors to match changed character to changed name.

So in a very real sense, this young boy's struggle to live was a struggle to regain his name. Could he survive the curse of being born in a land of famine and warfare and fulfill the promise of his name? The boy was no longer teetering on the edge of death, though it was far from certain as I sat perched on his narrow little hospital bed that night whether he would ever bloom again. The wounds—emotional as well as physical—were so very deep.

Jacinto awoke as I sat there thinking, and I prayed for him before I left the hospital that night. I prayed that he would feel comfort from the One who said, "Though father and mother forsake you, the Lord will take you in." I prayed that he would know "the Friend that sticks closer than a brother." I prayed that he would meet the One who values and respects life, who has given each of us an inheritance—by name—from the Father through the shattered life at Calvary. And I prayed that somehow our resurrected Lord would bring hope out of despair for this traumatized young life.

Another World Vision worker met Jacinto about a week later. He took Jacinto to the home of some friends for another month after hospital care was no longer needed, then to a rehabilitation center in Harare, Zimbabwe. Eventually, Jacinto graduated and returned to Mozambique, where he met a Man who understood his suffering more intimately than we can imagine—Someone who took it on Himself at Calvary that Jacinto could be set free from the torment of his past.

Through those who had befriended him, Jacinto was admitted to an orphanage near Tete. Here, he found people who loved him. He found new friends, understanding and security. Here as well he learned how to read. His first book was the New Testament. And his favorite verse was, "And He died for all, that those who live should no longer live for themselves, but for Him who died for them and was raised again."

Today—two years later—the promise of Jacinto's name is being fulfilled. He speaks with the confidence and peace that grows out of finding comfort in the midst of tremendous personal suffering. His smile radiates from a place deep inside where only Christ's love can touch—and where Christ's healing has restored a freshness that can only be compared to the morning bloom of the hyacinth.

The Scripture speaks of the Savior not breaking a bruised reed. In all my travels, I have met few who have been bruised as deeply as Jacinto—yet in the end, his injuries were not unto death, but to the glory of God. All who meet this boy are faced with a clear testimony of the healing power of God's grace. Jacinto will always walk with crutches, but the path he walks on now is filled with hope.

The curse of Chicaiba Maopa has been lifted, and the promise of the resurrection morning can be seen in a young man as excited and enthusiastic about life as a vibrant jungle flower after a cleansing thundershower. Christ's love has not only provided friends, a home and hope for the future, but has given Jacinto his name back as well. Let us remember their names.

Refugee camps are a blending of feverish activity and crushing boredom. For those whose task it is to care for the sick, the days are too long, the endurance too brief, the duties too many. For the sick themselves, days or even weeks often pass with little recognition of time. For the "healthy" (i.e., those not in immediate risk of dying), the days merge into a seamless cycle of boredom and hunger.

It's not a situation conducive to deep thinking or reflection, so it's not often we get the privilege of sharing in the thoughts and feelings of those in the camps. The next two stories, however, come from the Sa Keao refugee camp in Thailand, during a time when literally millions of people were fleeing the brutality of the Khmer Rouge. This first story is told by one of the refugees.

♦ ♦ ♦

Tonight, If I Die . . .

Just before dawn is the quietest. The tossing and turning has finally stopped, the low undercurrent of mumbling and groaning has ebbed to a trickle. Even the insects are temporarily silent.

It is then I can hear my heart most clearly.

Today, it tells me, will be better than yesterday. Today I have my name back.

Losing it was the ultimate indignity in a journey of humiliation and fear. First, we lost our possessions as the Khmer Rouge simply took what they wanted at gunpoint. Then they took our home, saying it was wrong for the country peasants to live in huts and the city people to live in walled houses. And then they took our city—telling us that Phnom Penh had to be evacuated.

I miss my city, my home, my family.

They are all gone. Surely the city remains, empty and soon overgrown as the jungle reclaims its own. My home? Who knows? My family? I cannot think of them. Not yet. All I know is that they are not by my side . . . I have lost them.

And until yesterday, I had even lost my own name. I was

11

but a body being washed along in a tide of bodies fleeing our homeland of Kampuchea. Some of us walked for months—I met one woman who, along with her child, had been sneaking along jungle trails in the dead of night for nine months.

You see, to move during the day risked discovery. And to be found by the Khmer Rouge meant certain death. Better to risk being eaten alive by the jungle animals than to be tortured and killed. At least the animals would have had a reason . . .

When we made it across the border here into Thailand, we thought we'd made it through the most difficult part.

We were wrong.

There were literally millions of us—Phnom Penh alone had over 2,000,000 citizens—who packed the secret trails to freedom. They tell me over 30,000 of us fill this one camp alone.

"Us"; by that I mean, "refugee." It is an ugly word. Even worse, for a long time that one word replaced all of our names. My name. I became less than I was at birth—at least when I was born, I was given a name.

I became "the pneumonia case with malaria near the corner pole." At least I was inside the tent. Three thousand of us were in the hospital compound, one hundred of the very sickest in the tent. On second thought, maybe it is not so good to be in the tent. My heart is unsure about this.

Yesterday as I lay here and listened to my heart, I was "Number 72." We had been given numbers instead of names. I don't think the nurses and doctor were any happier about this than we were, but they couldn't speak our language. Still, it didn't feel good to be a number.

Even animals have names. It is demeaning to be a number. Think of the tiger sliding through the jungle, his muscles rippling beneath his golden coat, fire in his eyes. Call him by a number? Not me.

Criminals are given numbers. Prisoners of war. But we are not prisoners, we escaped! Sometimes I wonder . . .

It is a terrible thing to lose your name, to be reduced to a number.

But today, my heart reminds me, I have a name again. My heart knew who I was, but only in the silent darkness before dawn could it speak it. Yesterday a man came all the way from Australia to speak for us. He asked our names, then gave them to those who care for us. Today, I am Meak once again.

Dawn has finally come. The gentle light filtering down through the plastic sheet that covers us begins to make people and objects out of the dark shadows around me. The nurse is here to check on me.

She called me "Meak." Her eyes glistened when she said it. My name was a great gift—it moved her to give it back to me.

My heart was right. Today will be a good day. Tomorrow, if I am stronger, I will ask her name as well.

Yesterday was the last day for burying numbers. Numbers 7, 71, 22, 34 and 68 were all wrapped in their ground sheets and lined up near the end of the tent. They were picked up and buried without their names. How terrible to lose everything, even your name. . . .

But the beds were filled with people last night, not numbers. There are always 100 of us. Some are cured, or at least pushed back from the edge of death far enough to face life in the camp outside—where not even a tent covers you from the daily afternoon rains. The tent is not really a tent, just a big sheet of plastic stretched across poles to keep the rain off. Those near the edge get wet, but they are closer to the breeze and can see the sky. It is hot after the rain.

Last night there was excitement nearby. I heard cries of pain and cries of babies. Che just told me that two new babies were born in the night. He says they are strong babies who will carry the future for the ones who have died.

Soldiers are here now. They are taking away our plastic

ground sheets and giving us wooden pallets to lift us above the mud.

Yes, this is going to be a good day. I am a person with a name now to the nurses and the doctor, and I am above the mud. No, there are really three good things, and the third is best of all—if I should die tonight, they will bury Meak, not just number 72.

These are the reflections of one of the nurses working in the tent with Meak.

◆ ◆ ◆

Refugee Is Not My Name

Millions fled across the border to escape the mindless carnage. Thirty thousand huddled together in this one camp alone. Few had made the trip over the mountains and through the lowland jungle unscathed.

Welcome to the Sa Keao Refugee Camp on the Kampuchean border. About 100 miles east of Bangkok, Sa Keao was but a leveled rice paddy carved out of the steamy tropical forest almost overnight in response to the overwhelming tide of refugees from Pol Pot's genocide.

When the desperate call came for medical help, I hadn't practiced in years. A few weeks of frantic review, and I was off to Thailand, with a quivery fear in my gut that I would be inadequate to the challenges I knew waited for me.

Once I arrived, however, there wasn't time for self-doubt. A steady stream of the sick and dying filled our days from dawn to dusk when the tide of darkness washed over the camp. There was no electricity to continue into the evening even if we'd been physically able.

15

With the night's quiet came a heightened awareness of sound. I'd collapse, exhausted, onto my cot, numb from the trials of the day. The close, oppressive heat seemed to carry even the smallest sounds. The labored breathing of the boy with tuberculosis. The muffled groans of the old man racked with malaria, parasites, pneumonia and perhaps five or six other opportunistic infections. The distant cries of a baby, or the mother whose daughter had been among the seven children we had buried that day.

I thought of the mother struggling with the burden of grief all alone in a foreign land, wondered what her daughter's name had been. And then it hit me—one of the most painful tragedies was our patient's namelessness.

"Refugee" was the only name we knew. The final indignity was dying in a strange land with no one even knowing who they were. In the end, they were carried off to mass graves, nothing more than another faceless statistic.

We couldn't speak Khmer. They didn't know English. We identified them by, "Third from left," or "The woman with the bed sores" or "The little girl with pneumonia." When we wanted them, we could only point and motion.

We tried a system of numbering each patient. It helped organize the pandemonium a little, but it hurt to call a vulnerable, suffering human being by a number.

And then—finally—the interpreter arrived. Now we could ask our patients about what happened, what their symptoms were, how long they'd been sick. And the faint security of having someone else know your name even produced the tracing of a smile on a few faces.

How wonderful I felt to treat Song, or Tim or Phe, not just number 95, or the tall, skinny boy with kwashiorkor (a disease produced by malnutrition and protein deficiency). And to discharge Cheng and Chin—even if it was back to the squalor of the camp. I wept when Chan and Meak died.

They weren't the kind of names I was accustomed to hearing, but they were the names their mothers had given them in great tenderness and by which their childhood friends had known them. They were the names shouted in greeting in the days before the horror came when they stopped smiling.

As we watched the change brought about in the hospital tent by using people's names, we, too, were changed and convicted. "Refugee" is not anyone's name. Each is a person who—just like us—needs to feel loved, sought after, respected, fed, clean, secure. Each is loved by the same God. The same Good Shepherd knows every one by name. Let us remember their names.

◆ ◆ ◆

The Marketplace

It looked like we were finally going to be able to leave. A premature monsoon rain that had hit Northern Laos held us hostage for more than a day. It was still raining off and on. But now 24 of us, sharing space with some caged chickens, a small deer and what surely must be most of a freshly butchered water buffalo, sat expectantly around the giant internal fuel tank of this vintage Soviet helicopter. Gusts of wind still rocked the machine from time to time as we waited.

The meat belonged to the pilot, and more than anything else, it encouraged him to take off in marginal weather. Blood drained from the packaging, painting the entire back of the plane a dark red. The meat would soon be rancid. Already it was ripening in the hot, humid air.

Just yesterday, I probably would have been nauseated by the sight and smell. But today, my relief at leaving the village of Xam Nau enabled me to shrug off my typically Western reaction to vivid sights and strong smells.

Until recently, there were no maps drawn for this part of the world. High, rugged mountains, often shrouded in mist, provided a navigational challenge for even the most experienced pilot.

Not that this area was not well known. This village, situated close to the Vietnam border, achieved critical importance during the long war between North and South Vietnam—for the Ho Chi Minh trail passed right through the heart of it.

The village people themselves had never been primary in the war effort. Never mind that every home in the village had been destroyed by American bombers a dozen times during the war. The village had value only because the land had value.

But that value ended 15 years ago, and today Xam Nau was out of the way, largely inaccessible, out of step with the world beyond the mountains and falling further and further behind.

We were here only because of bad weather. This morning as the rain had fallen with maddening persistence, we decided to wander through the marketplace to pass some time. No scheduled interviews, no strategic project analyses, just passing a few hours sloshing around in the rain because it was better than sitting in a musty hotel.

The humidity was high, even though the day was cold and chilly. Even inside, moisture formed on every surface.

We slogged through the ankle-deep mud to the center of the village where the outdoor market operated. I was surprised at the level of activity—apparently the rain had little effect on market day. Shiny wet children ran this way and that, shouting among themselves. Pigs squealed underfoot. Everyone had something to sell.

The sights and sounds were exotic, varied, a feast for the eyes and ears. But nothing impacted the senses like the smells. The soaking jungle provided the backdrop over which all other scents floated.

The condition of the people was represented by what they brought. A woman brought a bundle wrapped tightly in several layers of cloth. Freshly baked bread, still steaming, spilled out onto her laid-out mat and filled my head with its delicious, familiar aroma.

A farmer brushed closely by carrying a load of fresh vegetables, overpowering the bread smell with the universal odor of hard work and long hours in the field.

Nearby, freshly slaughtered pigs hung from overhead racks, the distinctive scent of raw meat competing with the warm bread and sweaty farmer. The next merchant held up a string of toads, still alive but skewered on a sliver of bamboo. Every few moments one of them would wriggle, not yet resigned to its fate. A proud fisherman displayed his catch, grinning toothlessly as he cleaned a large fish I couldn't identify.

The combined aroma of jungle, rain, mud, bodies, bread, meat and fish made my head reel. My stomach recoiled, not because any individual odor was so unpleasant, but they all pressed in so close. And the continuing rain seemed to drench me in the distilled perfume of the marketplace.

But what I saw next made me, I am embarrassed to say, stop and stare.

I stood there, stock still, mud oozing into my shoes, the rain dripping into my eyes and down the back of my neck and stared at what was for sale in the marketplace.

It was a dead rat, the biggest I had ever seen. It was stiff, legs sticking out at odd angles, the toes curled inward as if to grasp at something. The fur was patchy, and, like everything else—wet.

I must have stood there a long time, for one of the other people with me finally came up to see what I had found. He, too, just stopped and stared. Finally we moved on, splashing through the dark ooze that, later in the year, would become choking dust . . . .

My reverie was cut short when the helicopter pilot finally decided the weather wasn't going to improve any more and cranked the ancient engine. It started in a cloud of blue smoke and, after a few moments, we began the slow climb up to altitude.

One of the other members of our party, a photographer, started talking about his experiences at the marketplace.

"I saw you standing before that old woman with the rat a long time in the marketplace this morning, Bob," he said. "Did you see that face?"

His question pierced me to the quick. No, I hadn't seen her face.

I hadn't seen anything but the rat. Her precious humanity had gotten lost before the powerful images of her poverty.

Not only didn't I see her face, it never even dawned on me to ask her name. "You've still got a lot to learn, Seiple," I told myself.

I had seen poverty today. Smelled its odor. Felt its touch. But I didn't look it in the face.

Let us—dear God help *me*—remember their names.

◆ ◆ ◆

I Wish We Could Have Learned Her Name

The water was bad. The phones didn't work. Gasoline was in short supply.

It was hard to tell that Armenia's earthquake happened over a year ago. Narrow tracks wove through great piles of debris that once were buildings, spilling into the streets, turning them into an obstacle course. Leninaken looked like a picture of Berlin right after the end of World War II.

The landscape reminded me of Afghanistan with the rocky hillsides and snow-capped mountains. It is a land where the magnitude of the disaster still defies description. The sheer size of the land and the enormity of the impact contribute to a paralysis. This is a vulnerable area, with little but human grit and determination to fight the effects of a major catastrophe.

I was genuinely surprised at how little cleanup and rebuilding had taken place. Shelter was the primary issue. The winters in Armenia can be bitterly cold, and thousands still lived in the streets.

Gorbachev has said he wanted a full rehabilitation of housing within two years. If the progress over the first year was any indication, it may take a decade or more to fully transcend the overwhelming obstacles that exist for the people of Armenia.

The traditional building methods used in the area are extremely susceptible to earthquakes. Not only thousands of homes, but many of the large public buildings simply caved in on each other. The damage was far worse than it would have been here in the United States, with our stringent building codes.

My wife, Margaret Ann, and I were walking past a school to take some pictures of the "pancake effect." The violent shaking had reduced this school to nothing more than a massive pile of rubble. Apparently, cleanup efforts had not yet begun. It wasn't even clear whether any casualties had been removed from the huge mound that had once been an elementary school. I shuddered to think what the workers might find when the task finally began . . .

As we walked along what had once been a quiet side street, an old woman beckoned to us. Our western dress marked us as visitors. She apparently wanted to talk.

She was living in a steel packing crate, about eight by 25 feet, that had been moved in as a temporary shelter. It was typical of the housing we saw. Tents still littered the landscape everywhere we went.

A chill breeze blew what few leaves remained this late in the year into rustling, moving piles on the street outside. The skies were gray, leaden.

The woman beckoned us in. There was no door to close out the weather. The inside of the shelter was literally filled with beds. She had few possessions: a single-burner hot plate; some small oriental rugs attached to the steel wall; a small table.

She didn't speak English; we didn't speak Armenian. But we found that language was almost secondary to sharing a little companionship. She asked us to stay for coffee. On the little table were two pictures: one of her husband and the other of her daughter. Both had been killed in the earthquake.

Every time she pointed to the pictures, she cried. Great tears ran down the furrows in her cheeks.

Grief was obviously still a present, poignant part of her every day. Yet she must go on—the beds were for her six grandchildren.

We made some gestures to ask about the coming winter. "No mind," she seemed to say. She obviously had more to concern her than the problems to be faced next month.

The plumbing was outside. She carried in the water for coffee. We shared a small sweet cake. She washed some grapes and apples, and we spent a few moments "talking." There was no one left in her life except her precious little grandchildren— her best hopes, her closest friends were killed during the earthquake.

Given her age and her deep hurt, she will certainly carry her grief to the grave.

I'm not sure what she does with the kids. They must have been off to school. She can love them. Perhaps they were old enough to help with things "at home." The old woman's expectations were little more than a few moments of shared companionship with visitors, and maybe a few years of working for the children. There seemed little chance that her situation would change soon.

For me, she was a gripping symbol of Armenia today. The grief is profound. Hope is deferred. The expectations are small, short term. The fragile barriers between a harsh land and its people have been broken down, and a difficult life in a poor country became almost impossible.

Ethnic violence elsewhere in the Soviet Union has delayed building materials. Armenia is an ethnic territory within a socialist state, itself crumbling from within. As such, Armenia gets the worst of both worlds—overlooked and underrepresented by a centralized government which becomes increasingly ineffective the further one is away from the seat of power.

The rural areas seem to be recovering faster than the cities. I think this relates to the powerful sense of community evident in Armenia. In the large cities, high-rise apartment buildings are being built—a difficult environment in which to rebuild a fractured sense of family, of community. In the countryside, neighbors pull together to accomplish projects with common benefit. In the city, where we met the old woman, there are often no neighbors left. Those who survived left the ruins for the new apartments or were moved to temporary shelters.

We thought about giving the woman money, but felt like it would cheapen our relationship, make a mockery of what she had given to us. Her poor but warm hospitality and gracious welcome was beyond measuring with a handful of rubles. Instead, we thanked her. Prayed with her. Tried to understand her tears.

We came away with an acute sense of her individual suffering, her intense personal struggles to survive. Not even for herself, perhaps, but for the new generation committed into her care by a few seconds of panic and death.

Her dignity and generosity in welcoming strangers into her home, such as it was, was a powerful testimony of the human value retained even when possessions and most of the trappings of the modern world have been stripped away. I wish we could have talked. I wish we could have learned her name . . .

◆ ◆ ◆

I Hope You Will Grow

Vultures. Every picture I have of them is repugnant. Dirty, smelly, ugly, they reek with the stench of death and scour the land to pick clean the rotting carcasses of the fallen.

Especially in lean times, vultures become vicious competitors for food not only with other scavengers, but the active predators as well. Sometimes approaching four feet in height, their large, dull, hooked beaks and blunt claws cannot hold a healthy, active animal very well, but one that is injured or weakened has little chance of escape from the circling horde of death. And their ideal vantage point and keen eyes spot an injured animal long before the ground scavengers will.

Children are not the usual food of vultures.

But at the height of a North African famine—when the land had been almost entirely denuded by drought—a young man deep in the bush heard a child's hysterical screaming. He ran along the narrow footpath to discover one of the largest vultures he had ever seen feasting on a baby boy.

The hungry bird was not eager to give up its tasty morsel, but the young man finally drove it off and began his frenzied rush to get help for the baby.

By the time he got to the World Vision feeding center in Alamata, the tiny child was nearly dead. Deep wounds on his face, arm, back and legs were still bleeding. Vulture bites are ragged, gruesome holes where flesh has been torn out by powerful muscles rather than a razor-sharp beak. The baby was severely malnourished and acutely dehydrated. Despite their best efforts, the staff gave him little chance of lasting through the night. If he lived, they would decide what to do next.

To this day, we know nothing about his family or why, at the height of the famine, he was abandoned in the wilderness. The possibilities are all too horrible to think about.

Somehow, he was still breathing when the dawn finally came. The staff decided the baby needed a name, and they chose Biadgligne. In Amharic, the local tongue, it means I hope you will grow. The staff soon saw that this little boy had a remarkable will to live, a determination to survive that flew in the face of all he'd been through.

His new name signified that the past was gone with all its unspeakable horror, and the future is built on hope.

The scars are still plain to see. That probably won't ever change. But the inner scars are being healed over by Christ's love as seen through those around him. Against all odds, *I-hope-you-will-grow* is flourishing. His health is good, there's a twinkle in his eye. He plays happily with the other children. The nightmares come only rarely now.

Biadgligne is a powerful symbol. Literally hundreds of thousands of children and their families get stranded, helpless, along life's footpaths. And so often, their very survival depends on someone else coming by to lend a hand.

Most, like Biadgligne, will always bear the scars of their trauma. The loss of a baby, a father, a cheerful little girl or one's homestead leaves indelible marks.

But this lad's bright smile also reminds me that beneath the scars is the potential for health and wholeness. Our task is to help make it so, to recreate the miracle of healing across this world ravaged with sin and misfortune.

I hope you will grow. In a way, we give this name to every child we meet—every family, every community that becomes involved in the difficult struggle back toward self-sufficiency.

For if the hope for growth and transformation does not remain central to all that we do, we have forgotten the very name of our Savior. He stands not first as Judge, but as Deliverer. Not as Sovereign, but as Helper. Not as a distant Lord, but as God With Us.

And He's engraved on the palm of His hand our very name. For the forgotten, the oppressed, the hungry, the dying, the poor—let us remember their names. He does.

"Behold, I have graven thee on the palms of my hands."
Isaiah 49:16

Part II

◆ ◆ ◆ ◆ ◆ ◆ ◆ ◆ ◆ ◆ ◆ ◆ ◆ ◆

Making a
World of Difference

Ethiopia—photo by David Ward

♦ ♦ ♦

A Wedding Band

This is one of those stories that dates from the very founding of World Vision. I am reminded of it when I feel overwhelmed by the immensity of the problems we face today. The lesson I see is simple, yet profound: I am accountable only for what I can do, not for what I can't.

When that's not enough, my lot is to do what I can, then count on God to do what I cannot. The clearest illustration I see in the Scriptures of this principle is the moment when Jesus raised Lazarus from the dead. He told the people to roll away the stone—something they could do—and He called Lazarus forth—something only He could do.

God provides the vision; I provide the hands and feet. God stirs my heart; I respond out of my convictions. God opens the door; I step through.

Here's a story of the partnership between what we can do and what only God can do . . .

Solemnly and with a sense of great deliberation, the woman removed her wedding band. Especially in the time of

31

extreme hardship Korea was experiencing, such possessions were rare treasures. It was beautiful, the last remaining memento of her happy life before the war.

She pressed it into the hand of Bob Pierce (the founder of World Vision) with an admonition: "Take this back with you. Sell it, and use the money to minister to the pastors. My husband would want it that way."

So began World Vision's work among Christian leadership in the Developing World. That one woman's courageous and sacrificial act opened a whole new area of service.

The time was early 1953; the place, South Korea. As the North Koreans had swept down the peninsula in the early days of the war, they had systematically killed Christian pastors and devastated the churches. That woman's husband was a pastor and, as had happened to many others, their church was laid to waste. Thousands fled the troops' brutality. The Christian leaders who remained were overwhelmed in their attempts to minister to families and individuals who had lost so much.

It was clear that God's desire was to strengthen those whose lives were dedicated to His service. Without a miracle to begin the process, however, Pastors' Conferences seemed like just another of the unmet needs in Korea at the time.

This one woman's sacrifice changed all that. The shocked and deeply stirred American evangelist returned home with a new vision of obedience and example of esteem for God's house. The simple story ignited a new outpouring of support, and the first conference several months later hosted 300 pastors in Seoul, Korea, at World Vision's expense.

The effect on Korea's Christian community was profound. Pastors from all over the country learned to lean on one another for support and encouragement. Cooperative efforts in evangelism and personal witness sprang up. Resources, limited as they were, were shared in a united vision of building up Christ's body.

We often find it hard to comprehend the conditions under which Developing World pastors minister. Many do not own an entire Bible. Sometimes they cannot even read, but have been thrust into positions of local leadership by God's gifting alone. Especially in areas where there is little Christian activity, they may have no one to turn to for help.

Many full-time Christian workers in the Developing World make only two or three dollars a month. They cannot afford travel expenses for essential spiritual growth. Conditions are hard, both physically and spiritually. Pastors' Conferences serve this need.

Since that first gathering in Seoul, Korea, Pastors' Conferences have been held in more than 50 locations worldwide, bringing encouragement, teaching and fellowship to Christian leadership in the Developing World. More than 91,000 people have attended. The number of people's lives affected by the time of renewal cannot be estimated accurately, but we know it is multiplied many times.

There was no way that anonymous woman could have imagined how many lives her gift would eventually touch down through the years. Rather, she reached out to meet a need with the only resource she had. It isn't the size of the gift that God honors, but the spirit in which it's given. In simple humility and with no thought of personal advantage, a poor Korean woman's gift of love for her fellow Christians now reaches into people's hearts around the globe.

Few incidents can testify to the miracle of God's grace more than this demonstration that our mustard-seed faith and struggling obedience can be used of God beyond our understanding. Not always is the connection so clear, but I wonder sometimes how my actions today will affect the world tomorrow.

It may just be that you and I will take a step of faith today that will ultimately make a world of difference. This story proves it's possible.

From the very beginning, this ministry was founded on ordinary people like you and me —sharing what we could —meeting the basic needs of children and their families. Our growth and strength has not been in a few, big gifts, but in many little ones. This story helps take me back to our roots, confirms our heritage, and brings a new sense of perspective to my daily activities. In this sense, we are no different today than we were 30 years ago. . . . This story tells the background behind the first big donation we received. The time was 1960.

◆ ◆ ◆

A Wonderful Wealth

The envelope was just like the dozen or so others we had received that day. Nothing fancy, just a handwritten address postmarked somewhere in Wisconsin.

I slit it open and glanced at the name as I prepared to enter it in the ledger of daily receipts. This was not the most exciting part of my job—just a necessary routine.

But when I saw the amount, the hair on the back of my neck stood up. I rose to my feet without meaning to, knocking over my chair with a "crash!" An electric thrill seemed to pass up my arm from the check and all the way up and down my back. It was the largest check I had ever seen—and the largest single donation World Vision had received in ten years of ministry.

For several seconds, I stood there in mute astonishment. When I finally found my voice, I started shouting. "Hey, everybody! Look at this! Look at this!"

Soon the office was all abuzz with the news. Five figures! Nothing close to this had ever happened before. And it came at an especially critical time.

As the day progressed, however, I surprised myself with a churning cauldron of mixed emotions. Along with the feeling of joy and thankfulness, I felt something else, something vaguely disquieting.

I prayed later and began to understand a little more of what I was feeling. I prayed something like this: "Father, thank you for this wonderful gift. But—Lord, does this signal something different for World Vision? This work has been the wonderful multiplicity of many 'little people' giving little gifts to aid other 'little people' all around the world . . . Does this mean that now a few big gifts from a few big organizations will pay the way?"

My question did not get answered right away, but as the months passed, it became obvious that no such change was in the works. The check, it turned out, did not come from a big organization, but from a private couple. The couple who had sent the check had been faithful child sponsors for some years before we received it, and they continued on after. It seemed such an unusual situation, my heart kept coming back to it, wanting to know more.

Not until over two years later did I get the opportunity to find the answer to my prayer. I contacted the people and requested a few moments of their time. They agreed to meet with me. I had no idea what I would find. Such a one-time gift spoke of incredible wealth . . .

I arrived in a small town and followed my directions. As I reached the town's edge, I thought I might be heading to a millionaire's country estate. But suddenly I passed by an ordinary little bungalow with the right name on the mailbox. Surely it couldn't be the same people. Small town in Wisconsin; family names can be quite common . . .

Still, to be on the safe side, I turned around to check it out. I pulled up behind an old car in the dirt driveway of a humble little house indeed. I knocked on the door, expecting to find out that the people I wanted lived just a few miles up the road, behind the big gates.

A man opened the door and said, "Welcome. You must be from World Vision. We've been expecting you. Come on in!"

I was so stunned I was nearly speechless. "Mr. . . . ?" and I gave his first and last names.

"That's me," he said, and proceeded to introduce me to his six children. Yes, six children!

The oldest boy was blind.

Quite simply, I wasn't ready for this. All the prearranged questions and points of discussion just flew out of my head, and I had no idea how to begin. I guess I stammered around a little, the picture in my mind's eye of the check I had on my desk that day in such staggering contrast to the surroundings in which I now sat. But the family's warmth and obvious care for each other soon put me at ease, and the story began to unfold . . .

The man had been a tank driver in World War II. He had served with General Patton in the "Battle of the Bulge." He had seen the awful carnage of war, and how the children were the most affected of all.

The years between never erased the tragic pictures engraved in his mind of children crying by the roadside—pitiful hands reaching out for the least little scraps of food, chocolate or clothing from American servicemen. He ached over the thousands of orphans who would never again know the warm and comforting touch of a parent. Most of all, he remembered the tiny little ones desperately stretching on tiptoe for a few morsels of food from G.I. garbage cans.

When he returned to the States, he went to work in a local factory. His own children soon began arriving, but it seemed with each new baby of their own, his wife and he felt more deeply their desire to do something for the little ones of this world who had no one.

A factory worker's pay only stretches so far, but Christian concern is a powerful motivation. Along with the children who were learning to pray and care, the family learned to forego what they wanted in order that others might have what they needed.

An advertisement in a Christian magazine provided the vehicle to express their care, and they took on the monthly support of five orphans through World Vision.

And always there was in their own home a special reminder . . . their oldest boy. But he had the loving hands of parents to guide him—and thoughtful little brothers and sisters to be his "eyes," to share with him the wonders of the world around them, to help him "see" what they saw of this world which God had made.

Yet he reminded them of others around the world, less fortunate, groping alone through the endless and lonely night of their blindness.

They ached still to do so much more . . .

Their oldest son was admitted into a special school for the visually handicapped. It was too far to commute, so they had to sell their old house and move. They had built it with their own hands, and it was on a choice piece of land. The answer to their prayers had arrived.

The decision was simple. The new house needed only so much as a down payment. They had a roof over their heads, food on the table. Their home was filled with love and the presence of Christ—the comforts and conveniences of life could wait. They were content with such things as they had— and knew there were many more who had nothing.

So they decided to give to God the proceeds of the sale of their home. How? That, too, was easy.

They remembered the words of the Lord who said that anything done for "the least of these"—the orphaned, the widowed, the leprous—was really done for Him.

When the house was sold, they simply endorsed the check over to World Vision. For the least of these. For Him.

This was the check I held in my hand that day. The largest single amount we had ever received—but, despite its size, it was just another gift squeezed out of sacrifice. Given in the name of Christ by people who knew what need was like . . . but who were willing to give out of whatever they had to children who sob with need and heartbreak.

As I drove off in the gathering dusk, I stopped and looked back. I saw an ordinary-appearing little house, filled with an ordinary-appearing American family. But I saw more. Much more . . .

I saw a blind boy and his family who had learned to see the needs of others.

I don't mind telling you that I bowed my head over my steering wheel and wept. More clearly than ever before I saw the tragic poverty of riches apart from Christ—and the wonderful wealth that comes when you have nothing else but Him.

I saw a mother and a father who had given their children something infinitely more than those thousands of dollars—I saw parents who taught by example that their lives could make a difference in the lives of others.

And not just a little difference. A world of difference.

◆ ◆ ◆

When Old Dreams Die

Rarely have I had the privilege of meeting people who are so dedicated to their sponsored children as are Scott Sharp and his mother, Lily. Perhaps that is because, like children in the Developing World, they have faced daunting obstacles for which there were no easy solutions. They understand what it is to have deep needs only another can meet—and the unspeakable blessing of a hand reaching out to you in your darkest hour.

I have wondered, at times, how it is that God apportions suffering. Many of us know so little of it—others find it seems to dog their every step. All her life Lily had known suffering and struggle. I asked her to tell me about her most difficult time. As I might have expected, she did not tell me about her own pain, but that of her son. It all started with a phone call . . .

The telephone's jarring ring shattered the mountain silence. The voice on the other end said the words every parent fears. "There's been a car accident. Come home quick."

Instead of enjoying a much-needed quiet weekend retreat, Lily Sharp found herself rushing madly back to town and the hospital in Ann Arbor, Michigan. Scott, 20 years old at the time, had been hurled like a rag doll 80 feet through the air, suffering massive internal injuries and a punctured lung. He lay in a deep coma and was not expected to survive the week.

I don't know if she asked the question, "Why me?" on the way to the hospital. But I think I might have. She had never known what it was like to be part of a healthy, functioning family.

"We were dirt poor and my parents didn't want me. When they went out drinking at night, I'd sit at the end of the driveway and watch for their headlights. I'd cry and cry."

Because of her parents other neighborhood children were forbidden to play with Lily. "I remember pushing my nose up against a screen door, asking if another little girl could come out to play. Her mother said, 'No, she's busy.' But as I walked away, I heard her saying, 'I don't want you playing with Lily. Her family's trash.'"

Rejected at home and ostracized by playmates, Lily tried to earn love. At age nine she started cleaning houses. The money wasn't important—she would hire out for as little as 25 cents. What counted was being complimented on her work. "I was hoping I could be good enough to be accepted."

The situation at home grew worse. Finally at age 12, she was placed in an institution for homeless children, separated from the two-year-old sister she had mothered as her own.

Lily's desperate search for love ended, she thought, when she married at age 16. But as is so often the case when kids come out of broken, dysfunctional homes, the man she loved was but a tragic copy of her father, and he repeated the deadly patterns she had known as a child. He was critical, abusive and violent.

She decided to get the acceptance she needed through the only way she knew: cleaning. Clients commended her excellent work, and her janitorial business soon grew.

Despite a flourishing business and a young son, Lily's husband only got worse in his abusive ways. Lily tried to buy his love. She bought a house in the country where deer, pheasants and rabbits roamed along the creek that cut through the property. She paid off the mortgage in only four years, free and clear. Gift wrapped, she gave the title to their home to her husband for Christmas. It wasn't enough. Now he wanted a barn and $150,000 in the bank.

But when, some time after this, he demanded at gunpoint that she turn over her savings certificates, Lily had finally had enough. She filed for divorce. "I cried over lost dreams, the family, the love. I felt so guilty about the divorce, but in reality this man divorced me two weeks after we were married."

In the midst of the divorce, the phone call about the accident came. Everything she had lived for seemed to be slipping through her fingers. For more than 30 years she had tried to give love to a man whose only response was to brutally take anything and everything. Her one son lay on the edge of death. What good was a successful business when those you love are gone?

But Lily returned to the Rock who had gotten her through those many years. He understood both her anger and her pain. And now He gave her the strength to go on. When she finally arrived at the hospital, something deep inside her had changed—from crumbling clay to sturdy steel. Added to the compassion she had always known was a tough determination. She learned a new side of the Divine nature, saw anew the perseverance and grit that Jesus took through the garden of Gethsemane to the cross.

The doctors gave Scott little chance for survival. Lily simply said, "We'll see."

"I'd sit by Scott and say, 'Mama's right here. I'm not going to leave you.'" Lily knew what it was like to be abandoned, and she wasn't about to let it happen to *her* son. She'd tell him, "Jesus is right here, too. Remember Jonah and Noah and Daniel? God's going to deliver you just like them. I knew Scott heard me because he squeezed my hand."

The doctors said it was just reflex; Scott was still in a coma. But today, Scott will tell you different.

When Scott's survival was no longer a question of one day at a time, the physicians again told Lily that he would never walk, never talk, never eat normally, never even be able to sit in a wheelchair because of damage to his waist and hips. But Lily insisted, "I have a God who knows those hips and that waist, how they're made and what they're made of!"

The doctors were just as adamant that rehabilitation therapy was a waste of time. A full year after the accident, the conflict reached an impasse. Lily was despondent. One evening late as she was cleaning the local bank, she despaired, "God, it's been a whole year. If You're going to take Scott home, why let him suffer?"

She crumpled on the floor, finally digging out a worn devotional book. When she opened it, she read, "The purpose of his illness is not death, but for the glory of God. . . . Didn't I tell you that you will see a wonderful miracle from God if you believe?" From John 11, this verse gave her the strength to continue.

Fighting for the survival of her only son, contending with an abusive husband in the midst of a divorce and trying to run a full-time business all took their toll. Lily admits there are scars from this time. "When I look back at all the turmoil," she says, "I know there was the potential to become very bitter. But God was faithful. He said He would keep us, and He does."

Two months after this, Scott came home for the first time. Lily fed him strained foods, cared for his every physical requirement. Each tiny advance was the result of agonizing work. "You don't know, until you've been there, what you can do." Lily still refused to accept the prognosis of a complete, permanent disability. She hired therapists and recruited volunteers to work with Scott daily. Scott learned to roll over, to sit, to crawl and finally, with assistance, to walk.

But the most important advancement came when Scott learned to use a specially adapted computer to communicate.

One day last year, Scott wrote, "I want to become a missionary."

Now *that's* a challenge, Lily thought. Scott still couldn't speak or walk by himself, still spent his days in a wheelchair. Yet, there must be a way. After watching a World Vision special, they found a solution: what about reaching out to hurting people by writing letters?

Neither Scott nor Lily does things half way. So when the decided to become child sponsors, they did it in a big way. The Sharps sponsor 100 children, scattered throughout the world: in Asia, Africa, the Middle East and Latin America. Scott corresponds with each one personally.

The day I was there, they had just received pictures and biographical information on a newly sponsored child. As was his habit, Scott immediately began a letter to the child introducing himself.

A group of five letters flashed on the screen: "F G H I J." Slowly the curser moved over to highlight the "H." The computer beeped, and an "H" appeared in the box in the lower corner of the screen. A process that would last over the next several hours had begun.

Lily beamed. Scott's brow was furrowed in concentration as, with his one hand over which he had some control, he manipulated the control. After a long time, the screen finally read, "Hi. I'm Scott, your World Vision sponsor." I wondered if the child who would receive this, or the field worker who would translate Scott's letter, had any idea what a painstaking labor of love this simple note would be.

Scott finds purpose and direction in his ministry of correspondence. Lily talks about the fulfillment she now feels in her life. For the first time, she has peace in her home. She says that quietly, as one for whom old dreams have died—and new ones have been born.

She recently asked Scott, "Knowing what you know now,

that God could use you in that wheelchair for His glory, would you go through it again?" He nodded yes.

"I have to say the same thing," Lily says. "At the time, your heart's too heavy. But when you look back, you see how God's put each little thing together, even the things that were so hurtful. He makes you strong so you can do something for others who are hurting in the same way. That's what He's done for me. I guess that's really how you make a difference in this world."

I couldn't have said it better myself.

♦ ♦ ♦

Bridge over Rio Blanco

From one house to another the word flashed through the village: *The river is rising fast!*

Gregorio and his compañeros dashed out into the pouring rain to assess the danger. Assembled on the bank of Rio Blanco, they were a solemn group. The rain that beat down upon them dampened not only their hats, their necks and bodies, but their hopes as well. They watched helplessly as the raging water rose dangerously close to their precious bridge.

Gregorio remembered how the village had struggled before they had built the bridge. When the rains came and the river rose, the short walk to the market became a dangerous 12-hour trek over a winding mountain trail. The children couldn't go to school. Medical help became unavailable.

He remembered the times sick children had been unable to survive the long wait, or the times desperate adults or children had drowned trying to cross the river when the waters were high.

Gregorio smiled a little when he remembered the day the villagers had decided that they would build a bridge, and how they had managed to gather together $900 from the repayment of postearthquake loans. They were sure that was plenty of money—was it not twice what the average villager made in an entire year? But when the engineer came and measured and pushed some buttons on his fancy calculator, he told them the bridge would cost at least $5,000.

The village leaders had not slept well that night. What they had done without for so many years had now become so important to them. Gregorio knew they would never be able to raise that kind of money. They were poor, scarcely able to feed themselves. They had raised all they could.

The water had reached the bridge itself. Deep groans passed through the earth beneath them as the bridge strained against its anchors. The steel cables were stretched taut like rubber bands.

Many men had sweated hours carrying those cables over the mountain trails. Not to mention the 100-pound sacks of cement. But the villagers had borne the burden gladly, for their prayers had been answered. Christians from other countries had come to them, and had said they had heard about their desire for a bridge. These Christians said they were from a group called World Vision.

If the villagers would provide the manpower, World Vision said, they would supply the materials and engineering.

The bridge had taken months to complete. Everyone in the village had taken a certain portion of time away from their labor in the fields to work on the bridge. Just about everyone old enough to carry something had worked on it.

One of the engineers had asked Gregorio how high to put the bridge above the water. He didn't know, but together they had gone to the home of the oldest person in the village. "What's the highest you've ever seen the river?" they asked. Then, using the old man's answer, they had located the bridge.

Now Gregorio gazed sadly at the raging river. No one had imagined this would be a 100-year-rain. He looked at his friends. They should not be out here, he knew, soaked to the bone, standing in the cold downpour. But no one was about to leave. "Their" bridge was in danger.

This was the first time they had worked together as a village. Community effort was not something they had known before. Gregorio wondered if they would ever do it again. . . .

Suddenly there was no more time for reflection. A huge wave cascaded downstream, carrying tree trunks and masses of debris. It smashed into the bridge. For just an instant, it seemed to hold, then a loud crack filled the wet air and the cables snapped. The ground shook as the massive concrete footings were torn out. People began shouting and crying. Their precious bridge crumbled into the chaotic waters.

After just an instant, Gregorio leapt into the river. Eight men followed him without thinking about the personal danger. Somehow they managed to grab the steel cables in the bedlam of debris and drag themselves up on the other side of the river. They had saved at least part of their bridge.

Several weeks later, the men traveled to the World Vision field office to ask for help in rebuilding their bridge. "We saved our cables," they reported with great dignity. The village had decided to try again, and the men presented a letter signed by 46 of the villagers.

It was an eloquent testimony of the power they had seen change their lives by community action.

Had World Vision simply flown in technicians, construction workers and materials, the bridge wouldn't have meant as much to the village of Cimientos. The essential lessons of community organization and cooperation probably would not have been learned. Rather than giving them the bridge, we supported their own problem-solving efforts. The change in the tiny village has been dramatic.

The new bridge was built, six feet higher than before and grounded even more securely in massive cement footings. If anything, the work was more strenuous than before. But virtually the entire village shared in it. And now the village committee members are planning a medical clinic and literacy classes.

They'll need continuing help and resources, of course. But the changes in the community are permanent ones. The difference in their children's lives promises to be profound. They've learned they have the power to shape their own destiny.

Gregorio and his friends risked their lives to save what they could of the bridge in Cimientos. Now they are learning to give those lives in support of one another. No longer just a village of isolated, poor, struggling family units, Cimientos is now a community bonded together in the demonstration of Christ's sacrificial love.

Only if you've seen the difference such a project can make in a community would you really believe how complete the transformation has been. In fact, you might say there's a world of difference.

◆ ◆ ◆

When Darkness Gave Way to Light

Surely we've all been chilled before: covered with goose bumps on a gusty winter's day; eager to get back into the house to stand by a blazing fire, stamp our feet and hold up numb fingers to the welcome heat.

But not too many of us have been truly cold, dangerously chilled right down to the marrow of our bones. If you have, you never forget the feeling—hands and feet no longer just numb, but with a remote, achy feeling like they aren't really yours anymore. Afraid to look, hoping that frostbite hasn't set in yet, that the blood in your extremities hasn't yet begun to crystallize and destroy the very structures of life.

And if you *were* that cold, I wonder. . . . If someone asked you for the coat off your back to give to a stranger, would you peel it off?

This story recounts one of the most moving examples of selfless sacrifice I have ever known. And what to me is even more amazing, an entire congregation participated. It comes from the city of Taegu, Korea.

The time is 1950, six months after the start of the Korean War. One of the coldest winters on record has Korea in its icy

50

grip. Hundreds of thousands of Chinese regulars had poured across the frozen Yalu River just weeks before, completely changing the character of the war. United Nations and American forces were being routed. Miles of territory were lost every day.

Refugees by the thousands streamed south along the peninsula. As word of the atrocities being committed by North Korean and Chinese troops got out, the civilian population was in stark terror. Christian churches throughout the country held all-night prayer vigils. Predawn services for prayer and worship were packed in an atmosphere of siege.

Picture the situation:

There is no electricity, no city services are available. This is war. It's four o'clock in the morning, and today's service is just beginning. Inside this particular church, the temperature is eight degrees above zero.

It's dark and unbelievably cold. There are no chairs. Welcome. Pray with us. Pull up the floor and sit down.

The city is swollen with refugees. Tension and anxiety and fear are written on every face. Many in this room trudged over 200 miles from Seoul in the dead of winter, leaving just before the city fell to the invading army. Widows who witnessed their husbands being hacked to death gather their silent children close to them. There is great, great tragedy in this room, and poverty such as few of us can conceive.

Most are dressed only in thin, cotton-padded clothes. Women hold tiny babies tucked against their breasts, with such few clothes as they have wrapped around the children while they shiver stoically.

What can they be thinking as the service begins and they sing? The words are ones of comfort; the tears streaming down their faces declare both their need and their rejoicing in finding, in Him, the answer.

When the song service is over, the pastor begins to speak. He prepares to take an offering. What folly is this? What kind of offering could these people possibly give? They had watched their homes burn; many had lost every hope of an income of any kind. They were sitting in the bitter cold in desperate need. An offering? Why?

The pastor speaks. "Our offering this morning will go to the refugees who are still streaming into our city. They arrive here, as you know, with their clothes torn, shivering in the cold. Something must be done to help them. We must share with these our friends and brethren."

What have these people left to give?

The pastor continues, "And so this morning we will give an offering of clothes."

So that was what they had to give . . . *the clothes from their backs!*

Garment after garment appeared. One man, emaciated from his suffering, took off his jacket, removed his vest and laid it on the communion table. A mother took the top sweater off her precious babe, tucked the infant inside her own clothes to keep her warm, walked to the table in front and gave that one little sweater to keep some other child warm.

All they had were the clothes on their backs, and they were giving even these because of what was in their hearts.

John 1:5 says, "Jesus is the light of the world . . . and the light shines in darkness." That morning, darkness gave way to light. The faith that had gotten the people through thus far was rock-steady even in the midst of suffering and death—and was translated into a revolutionary demonstration of Christ's love.

The Marxist teachings that inspired so much hope in their adherents and so much fear in those they opposed have been shown to be tragically flawed since this story took place. The revolution we need is not one of political systems, but of the heart. Utopia, equality, justice—these are ideas precious to the mind of humankind but unattainable without a transformed heart and spirit.

Yet the grace of God provides us with the hope that

eternal changes can be brought about by flawed human vessels. Our vision exceeds our grasp, our hopes are not yet fulfilled, the evidence of our faith is yet unseen. But stories such as what took place that bitter winter morning of 1950 remind me once again that, individually and together, we *can* make a world of difference.

And what is making a difference?

"Is it not to deal thy bread to the hungry,
and that thou bring the poor that are cast out to thy house?
When thou seest the naked, that thou cover him. . . .
And they that shall be of thee
shall build the old waste places:
thou shalt raise up the foundations of many generations;
and thou shalt be called,
The repairer of the breach,
The restorer of paths to dwell in."
Isaiah 58: 7, 12

Part III

◆ ◆ ◆ ◆ ◆ ◆ ◆ ◆ ◆ ◆ ◆ ◆ ◆

Planting Seeds
of Hope

Ethiopia—photo by David Ward

◆ ◆ ◆

Mai of Ho Chi Minh

Alone in the midst of the crowd, Mai scans the faces of the arriving passengers. One by one they file past. Some are met by family, others hurry off alone. Finally the passengers are gone and the crew steps down the gangway, loosening their ties as they complete another long flight.

No, he is not on this flight. Maybe the next one.

She walks through the emptying terminal to begin her long walk back to downtown Ho Chi Minh City where the streets are her home. No, her father did not arrive today. Maybe tomorrow.

Yes, tomorrow he might arrive. She would meet the flight again. There is always tomorrow.

The airport personnel recognize her as she passes through the security checkpoint; they don't bother to ask her any questions. They stopped doing that years ago. They know that whenever there is an international flight, Mai will be there, checking to see if her father is arriving to take her with him.

Mai is an Amerasian, the daughter of a Vietnamese woman and an American serviceman. She has never met her father. She doesn't know his name, has never seen his picture. But someday, she believes he will come back to reclaim his daughter.

Armed with that unswerving hope, Mai has not missed an international flight into Ho Chi Minh City, formerly Saigon, since she was old enough to walk to the airport. And that has been most of her 22 years.

Mai's round, blue eyes and obvious American features ostracize her from Vietnamese society. Along with the thousands of other Amerasian children, she is an outcast, a pariah in a land whose memory is long and who faces daily, tragic reminders of the destruction of their land. The will and the resources to clean up the country have simply never been available.

America's involvement in the Vietnam war produced no victors, only victims. And while North Vietnam may have overpowered the South, they have lost the peace. A crumbling economy, stifling bureaucracy and international isolation have all conspired to further oppress a people who have known only civil war for generations.

Here in the U.S., we have "The Wall" as a reminder of our national pain and loss. In Vietnam, however, the reminder is much more personal. They have the Amerasians— about 30,000 children, now young adults, whose parentage can be traced to an occupying force and who have never been accepted in the land of their birth.

Like most of her Amerasian friends, Mai was forbidden to attend school and is not permitted to work in most businesses. Instead she works the streets of the city, eking out a scant existence on the very fringe of a crippled economy.

I met Mai at the airport the first time in April of 1988, during my first trip back "in-country" since I had served there in the Marines 20 years earlier. I was deeply saddened by both the lack of changes—I didn't see one new building, for example—and the changes that were sorely evident. What had once been a thriving metropolis was but a disintegrating monument to an earlier, healthier economy.

Mai occasionally sees her mother and younger brother. Her family bonds are not close. She's been on her own virtually as long as she can remember. She has only her hope to comfort her in the nights—and an occasional fellow Amerasian.

As I return to the airport several days later to leave, I think I see Mai's face peering over the barriers, once again scanning the arriving passengers. Perseverance is a part of the Vietnamese character. . . .

A year later I am again on an Air France 747 on my way to Vietnam, negotiating the final details of a new project in Da Nang in which we will be working with the thousands of amputees left over from the war. We have been invited back by the government, and hope is in the air for substantive changes. Not since we closed down the children's homes just days before the fall of Saigon in 1975 have we been able to work so constructively with the authorities.

Mai meets me once again in Saigon. She recognizes me from our conversations a year before and tells me excitedly that—after six years on the waiting lists—she has been accepted in the Orderly Departure Program. In two days she leaves Vietnam for Bangkok. After a week there, she will spend six months in a reorientation camp in the Philippines, then on to the United States.

I ask her if she is packed. "Yes!" she replies, and shows me a shoebox under her arm. Her life is contained in a shoebox.

I am thrilled for her. I have been to the camp in Bataan, Philippines, and know that she will find an intensive, well-balanced program of counseling, social orientation and language training to prepare her for her arrival in the "land of opportunity." I hope that, by some miracle, she finds her father and that he's glad to meet her.

I ache for her as well, for I also know the difficulty most Amerasians have in adjusting unrealistic expectations in housing, jobs and friends. America—where the streets are paved with gold, and acceptance, equality and brotherhood is the law of the land.

Yet Mai is a survivor. She's learned to be tough in the midst of her tears. Yes, she'll make it. Her hope will be tested, tried. Maybe even dashed for a while. But—as she's done for 22 years—she'll get up again. Because something in her heart keeps springing up new again, a part in all of us that declares there's got to be more than what we have now, what we can see and feel and touch.

My own son, Chris, was born within a few months of Mai in 1968. I was serving in the Marine Corps and was stationed out of Da Nang. The news of Chris's birth came to me via a Red Cross telegram posted on our living quarters' bulletin board. It was ten months before I finished my tour of duty and came home to be a father.

I am struck by comparing Chris and Mai. On the one hand, their lives have been almost totally disparate. Chris was virtually untouched by the war. Mai still lives daily with its consequences—one of its permanent victims.

Chris grew up enjoying a life of opportunities, of travel, of enduring friendships, lasting memories and family bonds. Mai has been a prisoner of circumstances, living on the streets without a father's love—both memories and possessions amply contained in a shoebox.

I don't know how to make things "right." I feel powerless to create either equality or justice. But as I look at them, I'm reminded as well by how much these two war babies have in common.

Our Lord loves them—a God who transcends geography, ideology and economic opportunities. Our Savior died for them. They are both part of the "whosoever" of John 3:16.

Perhaps the most I can do is to make sure that the Son of God is presented to Mai, in all of His fullness, just as He was made known to Chris. And perhaps that task belongs to each of us—to communicate the hope of eternal life to those who have experienced so little of life's fullness.

Hope is perhaps the most powerful, most enduring motivator I have seen among the poor of this world. Preserving and nurturing that hope provides a precious reason to continue their struggles to survive. But perhaps more importantly, we can provide the very seeds of hope to those who have lost everything—even a reason to face tomorrow. Bringing those seeds, planting them well and nurturing the sometimes-fragile plant of faith and perseverance that grows out of those seeds is perhaps the most important thing to which we can dedicate our lives.

◆ ◆ ◆

Operation Seasweep

Few episodes in history have been filled with such poignant stories of courage, loss and tragedy as the mass exodus of Vietnamese refugees during the late 1970s. The South China Sea was filled with tiny boats crammed to the gunnels with refugees and their possessions. Hundreds of ordinary fishermen became pirates, skimming off a rich booty of the small treasures the refugees had gathered over lifetimes. The real pirates brutally took what remained. And—unbelievably—the navies of some nations shared in the exploitation of the defenseless, naive Vietnamese fleeing the hardship of their native land.

Reliable estimates place the mortality rate at sea above 50 percent. Hundreds of boats simply scuttled when their few inches of freeboard were overwhelmed by the often choppy, always unpredictable sea. Some boats were so packed that there was standing room only for the long, hazardous voyage.

World Vision responded by purchasing a converted 300-foot freighter, the Seasweep, to rescue stranded refugees. Let me share with you the very personal story of triumph of Phong Ngoc Huynh and his family. His story tells of daring to believe in hope, its tragic

*loss and final restoration. The storyteller was among the first to
step aboard his boat when they were finally rescued.*

When I first talked with Phong, he hadn't eaten in five
days. He pointed out his wife and children seated in the stern
of the disabled boat. One daughter was covered with scabs
from the onslaught of sun and salt air.

"I have a brother in California. San Diego. Do you think
my family go live with him?" he asked.

The next day, after Phong had regained some strength,
he told me his story. . . .

Barely a ripple pierced the river's surface as the boat
crept silently through the dark night. Inside the noiseless hulk,
Phong, 27, huddled with is wife, Ank Ngot Tran, 25, their two
children and 285 other Vietnamese. The boat passed the river
outlet and began bobbing in the rough coastal waters of the
South China Sea.

Phong glanced back at his native land. "Will I ever see
her again?" he wondered. Sorrow at leaving the land of his
birth and joy at finally being free conflicted for supremacy in
his heart. Joy won—even to die in freedom on the sea was
better than living under the oppression his family had under-
gone. Just the possibility of realizing his hope of freedom and
peace was too precious not to reach out for it—even if it cost
them everything. Silently he prayed, "Dear God, please take
care of my family and my people."

They immediately turned south and headed for Singapore. The night and first day passed uneventfully. But on the
second day, a fishing boat rammed their small craft, crippling
it. The fisherman swept through the refugees, taking valuables, including Ank's wedding ring and the family's watches.

Four days later, unable to navigate, they ran aground off
the coast of Malaysia. Malaysian authorities herded them into
a barbed wire cage on the beach with 500 other Vietnamese
refugees.

For the first eight days, they received no food or water,
surviving on what they had salvaged from their own boat.

Eighteen days after they had run aground, the captors told them they were about to be released. They gave them supplies, then demanded what valuables remained. A Malaysian navy ship arrived, towing five small fishing boats. The refugees were divided into groups of about 100 each, then forced onto the towed boats.

"You're going to an island in the south," a guard shouted across the water to the refugees. The 30-foot-long open boat Phong and his family were on held 93 people. Its identification numbers and all markings had been painted over.

The navy vessel pulled away from the beach, the five dangerously overloaded fishing boats in tow. It increased steam until they were splashing through the chop at 15 knots. The little boats shuddered stem to stern each time they crashed through another wave. Spray drenched their huddled passengers.

After 20 hours of heading straight out from land, the Malaysians abruptly cut the ropes, setting the refugees adrift on the high seas.

The captain of Phong's boat protested he didn't have enough fuel to make landfall anywhere, much less Singapore.

"Shut up!" a sailor yelled back, then spun around the deck-mounted machine gun, firing a cascade of bullets just inches over the captain's head. Everyone dropped to the deck. The captain shut up. The navy ship steamed away.

The five refugee captains discussed their plight. Only one of the boats had enough fuel to make the nearest landfall, Indonesia's Anambas Islands. They chugged off.

The remaining four boats agreed to run their engines in shifts, two boats pulling two others in the hope they could conserve enough fuel to make land. Any land.

The plan worked for one day. Then the tired old diesel on Phong's boat quit, its injectors rusted by seawater in the fuel.

The pounding seas soon separated the four boats. Phong and the others tried to rig tarps together for sails, but the winds blew north back toward Vietnam.

The boat drifted helplessly for days. Water grew scarce despite rigorous rationing. Food supplies dwindled to nothing.

Twice they floated near fishing boats and begged for water and food. Twice their pleas were ignored. By the sixth day after this, the refugees huddled together in family units, waiting, as Phong put it, for the angel of death to arrive. One by one, they seemed to give up. The hope for freedom, so incalculably precious, was mocked by all this open sea. They were truly free—to die.

When the captain of *Seasweep* spotted the crippled boat through his binoculars, it had drifted back to within 120 miles of the Vietnamese coast. He turned the freighter a few points to come closer. "It's awfully small," he said. "Must be a refugee boat. It looks dead in the water. My God, I hope we're not too late." He ran the freighter's engines up to flank speed, and the ship surged through the afternoon swell. Agonizing minutes passed as the gap slowly closed. Vibration coursed through the ship as the engines strained to push it faster through the water. Sometimes even a few moments could make the difference between life and death.

The captain's eyes remained glued to the binoculars. Suddenly he spoke, "They're raising a white flag!" His voice cracked. "Two of them. It's packed full of people. They're alive!"

Suddenly the bridge was the center of flurried activity. Commands flashed off to the engine room, the infirmary, the kitchen. The crew prepared for every emergency they could think of. The refugees started waving. Reassurances were shouted over a bullhorn. Several of the refugees had heard about Operation Seasweep through a newspaper smuggled into their country.

"Our savior!" somebody yelled from the crippled little boat. Others joined in, chanting in hysterical relief, "Our savior! Our savior!"

As the two vessels pulled alongside, drums of sugar-laced water were hoisted down immediately. Stretchers followed in a few seconds. A limp 12-year-old girl was loaded on and was rushed off to the infirmary even as the refugee boat's captain was climbing up the ladder. A paralyzed old woman soon followed, then a dazed man, blinded as his tear ducts had dried up from dehydration.

Seasweep's chief engineer soon returned with the refugee captain to inspect their engine. *Seasweep* carried an extensive inventory of repair parts for just such emergencies. Tools were hoisted down. A long time later, the engineer climbed back aboard *Seasweep* and huddled with its captain. His diagnosis: seawater had seeped into the engine days ago. It would never turn over again. "Tell the refugees to gather their belongings. We've just inherited 93 new passengers," the captain said.

Too exhausted to cheer any more, the refugees clapped their hands in unison when they got the news. Those who could, smiled.

Vietnamese are fastidiously clean, even in abject poverty. So the refugee boat's condition declared as no words ever could the state of desperation in which we found them. The oily floor was awash in a vile mixture of urine, vomit and saltwater. When my bare foot touched the deck, my stomach lurched suddenly. The boat reeked. During their time at sea, these poor people had been reduced to living like animals.

I can't imagine how I would have survived those same conditions. Had I survived physically, the psychological and emotional roller coaster of high hopes, maltreatment at the hands of others and final loss of any belief that they would survive is unthinkable in normal terms. The breaking they endured is beyond my capacity to understand, or to feel with any sense that I am doing their struggles justice.

To brave the notoriously unpredictable South China Sea in a small boat, leaving behind everything I had ever known, only to venture forth into a world that doesn't want me—that defines for me both hope and desperation. I guess in the face of the lives they had known, hope is the only thing that gets us through. . . .

Phong and his family spent the first day aboard *Seasweep* either sleeping or eating—the lethargy of malnutrition and dehydration takes a few days to wear off. Not to mention the emotional exhaustion of teetering on the precipice of death for days and final rescue.

Within a few days, however, the refugees' incredible resilience was in evidence once more. The children ran pell-mell along the decks. Happy chatter among the adults replaced the deathly silence. Hope replaced resignation. Phong spoke of providing a good education for his two daughters, of improving his English, of using his training in the military as a mechanic once he got to the United States.

"I was an Air Force corporal stationed at Soc Trang, in the southernmost part of Vietnam," he said. "When our base was overrun we became prisoners. We built dikes for rice paddies. We were constantly called imperialists."

Phong was released from prison after only three months, but "freedom" was only a word. He couldn't travel. They were always hungry. And his family's running water and electricity were turned off permanently.

It took several missed opportunities before Phong finally set out to sea that night in their bid for freedom. With so many disappointments, how did he feel when he saw *Seasweep* and realized that he was finally safe?

"I was more than happy," he said. "There are no words to describe how happy I was."

He admitted that, in the last few hours before their rescue, hope had finally vanished. Resignation replaced a vision for a new future. They had struggled, dreamed, planned—all for nothing. The hardest part was looking at his two daughters, knowing he would never have the joy of seeing their lives bloom into adulthood, believing they would never know freedom. The most bitter pill of all was seeing the two young girls lose hope in life before they had really begun to live. . . .

When the *Seasweep* appeared on the horizon steaming directly toward them, they were so far beaten down that they didn't even dare to hope. Not until one of the refugees recognized the ship from the newspaper article did they stir from their macabre waiting for death to finally arrive.

But when the flame of hope was lit, it raced through the refugees like they were dry straw. And before the first barrel of water was received, the secret dreams of freedom and peace were already finding strength once again.

Phong had prayed much in that tiny boat, lost in the midst of a threatening sea from one horizon to another. But, as he shared with great tears in his eyes, his own faith had not been sufficient to see him through. It took a new seed of hope being sown. Short of salvation itself, that is perhaps the greatest miracle we see—new hope springing up from the ashes of broken dreams. The most precious seeds of all: hope in a new life.

◆ ◆ ◆

Terror at Sunrise

Two-year-old Aleixo froze in panic when he heard the first gunshot. He remembered the last time the bandits had come.

But this time they were not here to recruit or take supplies. They were here for revenge.

The shooting seemed to go on forever.

Aleixo watched, paralyzed by fear, as people ran screaming in every direction. The bandits gunned down everyone who moved—men, women and children.

At last the shooting stopped. Those who were still alive were herded together to carry off their possessions for the bandits, all except for a few of the men who were marched off into the bush.

Aleixo saw his father among them—with his hands over his head. Soon an automatic rifle barked in the distance.

Where was Momma?

Aleixo knew that his momma didn't see well. She suffered from nightblindness, caused by malnutrition. In the dim light of dawn when the bandits attacked, Mizelia saw only shadows.

She had searched frantically for her only son when the shooting started. But she couldn't find him.

Finally in desperation she had fled, hoping to save her two daughters, seven-year-old Catarina and one-month-old Marta. Mizelia collapsed in the long grass, weeping in frustration and fear. Why hadn't any of the shadows been her little Aleixo?

Her quiet tears stopped suddenly as she heard the bandits marching within a few feet of their hiding place. A man was pleading for his life.

She knew the voice. It was her husband.

His terrified pleas were cut short by a blast from a machine gun. Mizelia watched in mute horror as the dusty earth beneath her husband darkened with his blood. Within seconds, he lay still.

The early morning shadows had long since disappeared before Mizelia crawled out from her hiding place. The insects had already discovered her husband's body. Soon the scavengers would arrive.

Mizelia and her daughters ran deeper in the Mozambican bush, meeting the handful of others who had escaped the massacre.

But nobody remembered seeing little Aleixo.

Two scorching days and sleepless nights passed before they returned to what was left of their village. Little remained except ashes and painful memories. They began the long process of rebuilding their homes.

The second attack, days later, was as unexpected as the first. But this time no one escaped. They were too weak, too exhausted to run. The bandits gathered the survivors at gunpoint and prodded them into a grueling march north to their camp.

Mizelia remembers nothing about the many days they marched to the Renamo bandit base except her intense hunger and thirst. But their plight did not improve once they arrived.

They were left to starve, scavenging leaves and wild roots to stay alive. At night, Mizelia slept uncovered on the bare ground with her remaining children huddled around her, mourning her murdered husband and dreaming of her lost Aleixo.

She had no idea that he still lived—and how close to her he really was.

Only a hundred yards from where his family slept in the dirt, Aleixo was "in training" as a future bandit.

Death was not far off for Mizelia. Every day, the three of them were a little weaker, a little closer to being unable to attempt any escape at all.

So late one night, she led them off into the darkness. They headed east, hoping to reach safe coastal areas.

Mizelia recalls, "I walked day and night for a week, feeding my children on wild fruit and roots. It was terrible, carrying my little baby and trying to help Catarina. I had lost hope because I thought my son was dead."

They arrived in Quelimane, a provincial capital, after walking almost 200 kilometers. For more than a year, Mizelia lived in a garage with several other *deslocados*, people displaced by the war.

Food was scarce; they lived in unimaginable conditions, but at least they were safe from attack.

The Mozambican government finally moved them to a relocation center, where Mizelia was given about a half acre to cultivate. Alone but determined, she began living again.

She built a hut by hand out of mud, sticks and thatch. But like most *deslocados*, she had nothing to plant.

Help came in the form of an Ag-Pak from World Vision. Containing seeds, hand tools and instructions, an Ag-Pak gave a foundation on which Mizelia could provide sustenance for her children.

Her struggles continued. Mizelia's first crop was nearly destroyed by a drought. And what few rice seedlings survived were damaged by a cyclone when the rains finally did come. An invasion of locusts two months later swarmed over the ripening fields. She was as close to giving up as she had ever been.

Then . . . Aleixo returned!

Now four years old, he had been rescued after a bloody battle and taken to Quelimane. He lived there as an orphan for several months until an uncle happened to see him.

Nearly two years after the horror began, Aleixo was finally reunited with his mother and sisters.

Their lives will never again be the same. Their village is forever lost except to their memories. Mizelia's husband will never again walk through the doorway of the hut, but the simple provision of land, seeds, tools and training has returned something beyond price. She has hope once again.

Tomorrow's promise is still unsure. Mozambique's civil war has been stalemated a long time, and no one knows where the battle lines will be drawn in the future. But nothing is so resilient as the human heart, no quality so tenacious when it's supported as hope. Mizelia knows she has a long, difficult road to walk to rebuild her family's life. But she also knows that when she needs it, she has help to get there.

The seeds she plants are not only rice, but hope also. And she will reap not only grain, but a new life. When your whole world has been shattered by things you cannot control, hope, in the end, means far more than anything else. With it, anything is possible through God's grace. Without it, tomorrow will never come.

◆ ◆ ◆

Hope's Fruit

We have slums here in the West. They are places where the human spirit finds little to hope in, little room to grow into its potential. Most often, they are the oldest parts of the city, once prospering, now decaying. The passage of time and progress has left them behind. Once beautiful buildings crumble slowly in mute testimony to the broken dreams of the neighborhood around them.

India's slums, however, are beyond our darkest imaginings. The "Black Hole of Calcutta" was so named not out of exaggeration, but out of description. It is black not only in its dingy, grime-covered alleys and hovels, but it is black in the deepest depression, hopelessness and perceived human worthlessness known on the planet.

For a hundred generations, human beings have been born there. They eke our a pitiful existence for a few short years, and die there. The caste system further represses any hopes of change. Being born as an untouchable was an irrefutable statement of horrible sins in some past life. There was no hope of changing one's lot in life this time around. The best to be hoped for was to die young in the expectation of coming back a superior, more worthwhile being than such a low caste. A cow, maybe.

I thank the God who created us all in His own image, however, that such bondage is no longer a *fait accompli* upon the moment of one's birth in even the darkest Indian slums. That there is hope even in the most deplorable slums is shown clearly in Sudanthira Devi's life.

Twenty-two years ago, Sudanthira was born into a family living in desperate poverty in one of India's most notorious slums. She had virtually no hope of an education or any opportunity to break the chains of her family's multiple-generation destitution. But a child sponsorship program changed all that. Committed child sponsors in the West enabled her to receive basic living necessities and a primary education. Eventually she earned a university degree. Sudanthira was determined to escape the destitution that had characterized her own childhood and her parents' entire life.

Armed with a degree, Sudanthira could have chosen virtually any field of endeavor. She chose to go back to the slum as a social worker.

Today she works in Madras in a neighborhood so wretched and filthy that even other slum dwellers look down on it.

Why would she return to the very environment she worked so hard to leave? "Because I know from my own life what a difference it makes when someone reaches out," she says. When, as a young child, she was foolish enough to dream of a life free from hunger, deprivation and the constant threat of a disease-ridden death, substance was added to those childhood hopes.

The seed of hope is resident within all of us. We work to create an environment in which it can grow before it is crushed by deprivation. In the most desperate of circumstances, this intervention must begin at a young age. Sudanthira's understanding of this urgency focuses her work in the slums. She spends her life giving back the hope she received from the hands of Christian strangers. "I'm especially interested in ministry to children," she says, knowing firsthand how God's love can enrich a child's life.

The value of breaking the cycle of childhood sickness, lack of education and the resulting sentence of lifetime poverty is seen in Sudanthira's own son. He lives in a world today far removed from that of his mother's childhood.

And the difference is really nothing more than planting the seeds of hope, then nurturing them over a lifetime. In this case, as in thousands of others, the fruit is already being passed on to another generation.

♦ ♦ ♦

Children of the Dump

We stood on the roof of our child-care center just outside the Guatemala City dump. Acres upon acres of steaming, smoking refuse spread out before us. When the breeze spun around the compass and we were downwind, the stench was overpowering. I gagged involuntarily.

Several times the whole scene was blotted out by the thick, fetid smoke that bit my throat and assaulted my nose with its sharp pungency. Fire blazed openly in some areas, smoldered everywhere, burning through rotten meat, industrial chemicals, spoiled vegetables, household trash.

But not before an army of children picked through it for the least little thing of value. The city's garbage trucks maintained a constant stream down into the pit. As each one arrived, the children swarmed to it like fish in a tank gobbling up food.

A young boy and girl caught my eye. They acted like brother and sister, picking carefully through the garbage that is their life. Suddenly the boy grabbed the little girl by the shoulder and pointed. The bulldozer had uncovered something. Their pace quickened, and they were not quite so cautious.

Other children had seen it as well. From two or three different points, they bolted toward it. The boy and his sister broke into a run, throwing caution away in a desperate race. They moved with amazing quickness. It was literally a race for survival. There were no second place prizes. Only the swift and cunning would eat tonight.

The boy reached the prize and began feverishly pulling at it. His sister arrived a second later, chest heaving. Between the two of them they managed to loosen it just before the other children arrived.

It was theirs. They scurried off to redeem whatever it was they had found.

They were truly pitiful to watch—faces and bodies encrusted with dirt, open sores running down their arms and legs, teeth broken and missing, hair matted and filthy.

I find it incomprehensible that children are allowed to live like this. The only thing bright and clean is the sparkle in their eyes. And even that will be gone before too many more years will pass.

But in their eyes still flickered the spark of hope—that part in all of us which invites us to commune with our Creator.

That children could spend their days in such a place shocked me. That entire families live within the borders of the dump—are born there, raised there, have children there and, eventually, die there—disturbed me profoundly. I was told there are people in the dump who have never been outside its gates. Not children. Adults. Their whole life has been scavenging through another's garbage.

One of the others who watched with me observed, "They were in the dump, and the dump was in them."

I think the thing that distressed me the most about the scene was that all the value was in the garbage—no value was placed in the human beings whose pitiful survival it is to pick through it.

Despair, hopelessness, overwhelming pathos, spiritual warfare were as thick as the smoke itself. The forces of darkness, death and sin were strong in that place. I understood very clearly Jesus' metaphor of Gehenna—the dump outside of Jerusalem—as an apt description of hell. Before me stood hell on earth! I struggled with both the immensity and intensity of it.

This was a dangerous place. The police refused to enter. The turf was controlled by strong-armed thugs who profit from the children's and families' labor.

I thought of a hundred things we needed to be doing to minister to the needs of the children and their families living in the dump. But the longer I watched, the more I became convinced that I was in the midst of intense spiritual warfare— that the real crisis in the lives of the children and families below was not education, or health care or nutrition, but hope.

The miracle we needed was not one meeting natural needs—important as they may be—but the supernatural, the eternal. The spiritual warfare going on in that dump had to be won first. Hell is only transformed by the power of a risen Savior.

Hope is not a concept that is easily understood at the dump. Those who lived there did not experience it. The young knew of it, for hope grows naturally in the human heart, but the seeds of it are so quickly snatched away by the dark environment. So little light shines into the hearts of those imprisoned there by circumstance.

I am reminded of the passage in the Psalms which says, "He drew me up from the horrible pit, out of the miry clay, and set my feet upon the rock, making my steps secure" (Psalm 40:2). Christ is the One who must reach down into the pit and deliver its residents. We cannot expect them to climb out on their own—for they do not even see that it's possible.

I am humbled by the dump. But I also know that the One who delivered me from my own spiritual blindness, who caused me to see, and feel, and experience hope—can do it for the children of the dump as well. And as we allow Him to work through us, He can also provide the insight, the energy, the perseverance to overcome this hell on earth.

The trashy prize that spawned such frenzied activity that day was a thing of great value to the children of the dump. But God does not see as we see.

The treasure was not in the trash, but the children.

We must redeem them. It can be done. The seed of hope is already there—I saw it in their eyes.

◆ ◆ ◆

Hopscotch

The telegram was as brief as it was shocking. "Have found pocket of 35,000 *deslocados* in Gile. Suggest you come." *Deslocados* are refugees, the "dislocated ones." Finding that many where no relief programs operated promised that this would be a difficult trip indeed.

As the sender of the telegram well knew, changing itineraries around in Africa mid-trip is sometimes impossible, so this was a serious request. We managed, however, to make the changes to go to Gile, Mozambique.

Mozambique has been embroiled in a bitter civil war virtually since its independence from Portugal in 1975. Once a rich and fertile land, the country has been ravaged by warfare, and it is now one of the poorest places on earth. Recorded casualties in the last few years exceed 100,000, and recent changes in weather patterns have crippled traditional food production. The United Nations estimates that nearly six million people in Mozambique need relief assistance.

Until just a month before our trip, Gile was held by Renamo, the rebel group. As we circled the town on final approach, I could see the destruction the rebels had left behind. Only one small building had a roof left on it. Virtually the entire town, a district capital, had been destroyed.

When we landed, entire families flocked to the airstrip. From 50 yards away, I could see their bones protruding. Their clothing consisted of burlap bags and bark. Malnutrition was obvious in about one third of the inhabitants. And once you can see it, malnutrition has become life-threatening.

The only food was cassava. All starch, it provided little to live on. Some 300 people were dying of starvation every month. Ten people every day wouldn't survive to see another sunrise.

It was the most heartbreaking scene I had ever witnessed. I met so many whose stories tore at me. . . .

I met a young mother in nearby Mocuba named Julietta Mubiana. She had been captured by Renamo and held along with her two sons, Joal and Daniel. Julietta had advanced tuberculosis. Her remaining days on this earth were few.

When the three of them were captured, Julietta was beaten as her sons were forced to watch. Then, the boys, still standing by in impotent terror, watched as she was raped. Any soldier in the band who wanted was encouraged to casually, brutally, repeatedly take whatever twisted pleasure he desired with the diseased, broken and bleeding woman. All this while her sons watched.

This continued for many days. Just before she was let go, they beat her legs and the soles of her feet. As she hobbled away from the rebel camp, there was agony in her every step.

How she made it to the camp I don't know. Somehow she found her husband and third child there, so at least they were together. Julietta was nothing but a skeleton. What the lack of food did not take away the tuberculous did.

It was ironic to me that Julietta fled her personal nightmare, only to land in Mocuba—a reality worse than any dream could be. Yet to talk to those in the town, the brutal caprice of the war was more to be feared than simple hunger.

I was struck by how so many people could gather in such desperate straits and nobody know they were there. The civil war in Mozambique has victimized virtually an entire country, yet still I am amazed that a catastrophe of such proportions could exist without the outside world knowing anything about it.

Yet a more moving image to me than the thousands of unknown victims was found when wandering the streets of Gile. In the middle of thousands of *deslocados* in the midst of a guerrilla war zone and untold suffering, I saw the faint outline in the dirt of a hopscotch game.

Hopscotch. A harmless, innocent diversion for children. Children who somehow managed to focus their attention not on their aching bellies or bleak future, but, for a few minutes at least, to play.

I found that tremendously encouraging. For I've seen that when the children stop playing, hope is lost. That faint diagram in the dirt meant that hope was still alive. And where hope was, anything was possible.

That was two years ago. Sad to say, many of the people I met have since perished. But the children's hopscotch game continued, and as a result of seeing their desperate plight we mounted a massive emergency relief effort. Tons of food were flown in; literally thousands of people were fed every day. Only God knows how many lives were saved.

I can't say that finding that hopscotch game really made any difference in the way we responded. But I do know it made a difference in me. For if a little girl could have enough hope to play a game of hopscotch, couldn't I do whatever it took to sustain that hope, to preserve her life?

I'll never see another hopscotch game scrawled in chalk on the sidewalk or scratched in the dirt in quite the same way. For me, it's become a powerful symbol of hope from a land where little hope survives.

I wonder, is there any significance that the game squares form a cross? Perhaps the game pieces themselves, be they twigs or stones or coins, become a kind of seed for hope in the hearts of those who play it.

The next time I visit a refugee camp, I think I'll ask a foolish question: "Tell me something. Do the children play hopscotch here?" If they do, I know the seeds of hope have already been planted.

◆ ◆ ◆

The Most Priceless
Seeds of All

For weeks Waji Chefraw had rationed his last basket of remaining grain. The loaves of *injera,* the flat bread with which they ate every meal, grew smaller and smaller. But today, even the *injera* was gone.

Waji covered his eyes and peered at the deep blue sky for a cloud, even the suggestion of one. He knew it was fruitless— no rain had fallen now for two years. But one could always hope.

His home was in the foothills overlooking the Ansokia Valley. In good years, it was lush, productive farmland. This year, however, twisters of dust rose high into the dry air, dancing across the brown and desolate valley. Heat waves made the hills on the far side of the valley shimmer. The bones of fallen livestock littered the parched earth.

Since he was a little boy, Waji had known seasons of plenty, seasons of hunger. But this time, not even the hyenas had enough to eat. He had heard them coming down out of the mountains at night and knew if they decided his family was to be their next meal that he did not have the strength to fight them off. Were not his children already so listless from hunger and malnutrition that they rarely left their hut, he would have forbidden them to play more than a few meters away from their home.

Waji didn't know what to do next. If there was no food here, one of the richest, most productive valleys in Ethiopia, there was no food anywhere else. Maybe they could make the 200-mile trek south into Addis Ababa, the capital. Surely no one would let them starve there.

Then again, hundreds of people had already died from diseases that swept through with unusual virulence. Waji had only a vague understanding that, as so many had cut back on their food intake so drastically in the hopes to last out the famine, they had also weakened their resistance to disease. Any infection is made much worse by malnutrition.

All day, Waji had been wondering at the growing number of people he could see crossing the valley. By the afternoon when he, his wife and five children ate the last tiny loaves of *injera*, the air had grown hazy with the dust from hundreds, perhaps even thousands, of feet.

Hulita, his wife, and Waji talked late into the night. They agreed that they could not just sit here and starve. Perhaps there was food at the other end of the valley. Perhaps that was what was drawing so many people.

With the dawn, they gathered the children and started off. Four were old enough to walk. The youngest had to be carried. There were no roads to follow, only an indistinct but growing conviction that there must be food *somewhere*, even if not here.

Their pace was slow. The younger ones' bellies had begun to swell weeks ago as kwashiorkor, a protein-deficiency disease common among the malnourished, set in. Within a few hours, however, they had heard the news.

There was food. There was hope.

An emergency feeding camp is not a place you or I visit without a little preparation. It is not a place for the weak of heart—or stomach. During the height of the famine, 15 to 20 people—mainly children—died every day. Many arrived in tattered rags, exhausted from journeys of a hundred miles and more without a scrap of food.

The most pitiful collapse just as they have finally reached their destination—too weak to lift a lifesaving cup to their lips. Parents walk silently up carrying the child who died that morning, mere hours away from salvation. The worst is when they don't know it yet—for the babe has been listless and unmoving for perhaps days. Imagine the agony of finally finding food and water only hours too late.

Ansokia went from a native population of 25,000 to more than 60,000 as the word got out, *"There's food!"* Transportation presented incredible obstacles. There were simply no roads into the valley. Those who could still work stamped out a gravel landing strip for supply planes. A train of 1,000 camels hauled in more food and medical supplies. For many months, this massive effort continued. The compassion of the world was poured into remote and previously unheard of little valleys like Ansokia. For the first time, famine, poverty and starvation became front-page, prime-time, lead story news.

And as a result, Waji and his family survived.

By the spring of the 1985, many people were well enough to begin to return to their homes. The first hint of moisture had fallen in over two years, and the land once more made its eternal promise of green.

Over the last 250 years, however, Ethiopia has averaged one famine every seven years. The rains would fail again, and as the population increased, so too would the consequences of any harvest shortfall. The famine of 1984, we began to understand, was but a bitter foretaste of the unspeakable disaster that awaited Northern Africa if something was not done quickly.

The undeveloped nations of the world are littered, however, with the rusting hulks of well-meaning development efforts and their equipment. Yes, diesel tractors and chemical fertilizers could multiply Ansokia's food production a hundredfold. But just as surely, it would return to dust as soon as the experts and technologists left.

The challenge became to create a model of locally based famine-resistant development, utilizing the skills, priorities and motivations of those who lived there. Unless the people themselves understood, desired and participated in the program, it was but a massive waste of resources and time.

And time was something in short supply. No one knew when the next big famine would hit. It might wait seven years, perhaps only two or three. But the next time, a massive response by the world's wealthy nations like what was witnessed in 1984 was anything but assured.

So World Vision development experts met with village leaders to determine what their long-term needs were. The list was easy to outline: reliable sources of clean water, improved crop production, basic health care, some way to control the erosion that destroyed the hillside fields, and trees. Lots of trees.

The old-timers remembered when the valley and hills were heavily forested. But as the population grew, so too did wood use for fuel and construction. By 1984, only a few little gnarled fig trees remained out of an entire forest.

So as the villagers led their own people, we came alongside with resources, expertise and education. The project was funded by donors in the Developed World, but the soul of it was securely rooted in the hearts of those in Ansokia Valley.

The changes wrought in Ansokia are nothing short of miraculous. When once tons of food had to be flown in, now Ansokia exports food. Where once barren hillsides lay open to windblown erosion, now literally millions of young trees declare a reason to hope for tomorrow. More than 120 miles of stone terracing prevents destructive runoff from the hills. Water management techniques and appropriate agricultural science are now taught by local village leaders who have become experts in their own environment.

As it turned out, the next famine did not wait seven years. Only two years after the rains returned, they failed again just as suddenly. But this time, Ansokia Valley was ready. Deep wells had tapped the abundant aquifer under the valley floor.

Drought-resistant grains grew with less water. Crop rotation allowed the fields to be productive throughout more of the year.

This time, a central feeding station importing food was not necessary. The pattern of disease, famine and starvation has been broken. The rains may still fail, but the food supply will not.

Waji Chefraw and his family have returned to the home they left so soberly years ago. Many of the trees he planted are already 30 feet tall. Their shade is a welcome retreat on the hot summer days that will always be a part of North Africa.

Hulita still makes *injera* every day. Life is still hard. The labor is all done by hand, as it has been for countless generations and will continue to be in the foreseeable future. For you see, development that truly benefits the community must spring up from its midst, out of the beliefs, convictions and priorities of those who know their needs best.

Their task is to provide the initiative, the commitment, the labor. Our task is to provide what they cannot: the resources, the expertise, the technology that can be supported and maintained by local artisans and craftsmen.

Seven-year-old Sisay, barely old enough to walk with his father Waji when they made that fateful journey to the World Vision feeding station in 1984, has climbed high up in their papaya tree. The fruit is ripening in the hot sun, and the sweetest ones are at the very top.

Hulita chases a cow out of the onion patch. Waji takes a break from his task, wipes his sweaty brow and surveys the valley.

No dust devils dance among skeletons today. Instead, fish ponds glint brightly in the distance. A church the villagers built to worship in sits alongside the new road that runs through the valley. Terraced acres of green cover the valley floor. The darker green of trees carpets the hillsides.

The people have worked hard for the changes Waji sees, and he has been a part of it. Countless hours of backbreaking labor can be counted among the cost to transform this valley.

But the price has been worth it—more than worth it. Because the fruit of it has been more than food. It has been hope. Nothing declares that more clearly than the new family of God that is growing throughout the valley.

For the first time ever, Waji knows that his children will have enough to eat this year, and the next. The seeds planted the day the family left in a desperate search for survival have borne fruit. For not only have they borne hope, but confidence. Confidence in God's grace. Confidence in his own ability to care for his family. Confidence in their worth and value not only as human beings, but as God's children.

The seeds of hope bore the fruit of faith. And that makes them the most precious seeds of all.

"And hope maketh not ashamed:
Because the love of God is shed abroad in our hearts
by the Holy Ghost which is given unto us."
Romans 5:5

Part IV

◆ ◆ ◆ ◆ ◆ ◆ ◆ ◆ ◆ ◆ ◆ ◆

One Life at a Time

Honduras—photo by Nancy Kyle

◆ ◆ ◆

One Small Boy

His head rested on an outstretched arm, palm up in the dust. Even in sleep, the little boy seemed to be asking for help.

The dirt on his face was streaked. His hair was long and unkempt. His clothes were ragged. He couldn't have been more than about eight years old.

It was the end of a long and busy day just after Christmas of last year. We had met with village leaders throughout the countryside of Honduras, planning a large project that would benefit thousands of people. We had just had dinner and were exiting a small restaurant in the town of Choluteca, a dusty, dirty little hamlet in southern Honduras. And right there in front of us was this little boy, sound asleep in the dirt.

We were instantly uncomfortable. We stopped, gazed at his sleeping form and quiet, agonizingly young face and, being careful not to wake him, stepped over him, crossing to the other side of the street.

There, we gathered to discuss the situation among ourselves. Our host said, "There are a lot of children like this. It is a real problem in the city." The subtle message was there are so many, don't be troubled about only one. He was part of a much larger generic problem, a problem endemic to Choluteca. The plight of this vulnerable little boy, an individual, became depersonalized as he was folded into the larger issue facing this small town. We assented, and went on our way.

We made a mistake.

A few days later as I participated in a time of biblical reflection, the teacher began the lesson with, "There is very little more that can be said that has not already been said about the parable of the Good Samaritan." My immediate thought was, *Fine. It's all been said. Maybe we should stop talking and start doing.* But with a piercing pang of conscience, my mind and heart went back to our experience with the little boy only four days earlier. I was reminded that the lessons in the parable are learned slowly, sometimes with great difficulty, and apply to me today.

The Samaritan was an outsider, a stranger who saw the situation with a fresh perspective. Locals knew the area was infested with highwaymen. They had probably seen victims beside the road many times. The Samaritan did not see the class of "victims of highwaymen" though. He saw an individual.

So too, in Choluteca, our hosts had perhaps seen too many little boys sleeping in the dust in front of the restaurant. But that evening, we did not step over a class of "sleeping boys," we stepped over an individual. One, I believe, that God placed directly in our path.

It hurt to realize, like the Levite in the parable, we crossed over to the other side of the road. We managed to quell our personal disquiet and go on our way to our hotel for the evening.

The magnitude of the problem becomes paralytic when we see not individuals, but classes. So often we refer to Matthew 25 which speaks of "the least of these." But we forget just one little word: "*one* of the least of these." God never expects us to do everything. He does ask us to do something.

Children are born, live and die one at a time. We must likewise care for them one at a time. Mother Teresa has said,

"God has not called me to be successful. God has only called me to be obedient."

For us that evening, the question of obedience—the instant response of our hearts—was tied to one small child. To the diminishing of all of us, we managed to step over both our hearts and the boy.

I am convinced that, were we to listen to that still, small voice of compassion within us when first it speaks, our actions in our day-to-day world would be much different. Yes, that voice, that first response of our hearts, was an interruption.

But so much of Christ's ministry took place at points of interruption. That day in Honduras, we were drawing to a close a well-structured, productive, busy day. We had a similarly scheduled day in front of us. There was much to accomplish in the tight time line allowed. We were so busy doing the work of God that we had no time for the things of the Lord!

The conscience is convicting. It cares not for schedules, sees not classes, responds not out of a listing of projects and priorities. As the very testimony within us of God's love, it sees instead individual lives, hearts and needs. The conscience looked on the face of that sleeping boy, and cried out, "Help him! Now. Do what is in your hand to do. Reach out with whatever resources God has given you to accomplish the tasks He has set before you." We were not asked to minister to all the homeless boys in Choluteca, just one.

But because of the many, we missed the one.

We had money. An "inn" was just next door. In fact, we were headed there ourselves. We could have been the perfect good Samaritans. But we let the persuasive arguments of the world set aside the heart of God.

I tossed and turned all night. The outline of the boy in the dirt kept filling my mind's eye. The profile of his face, dark hair sweeping across a mud-caked cheek, kept reappearing before me. I imagined his open hand reaching out to me, and I walked away.

I was up at dawn and, like the king who wanted to see if

Daniel had survived the night in the lion's den, hurried down to the street.

The boy was gone. Not even an impression in the dirt remained.

The opportunity was lost. The only obedience left to minister to that little boy was to pray.

It did not feel like nearly enough. I was angry and frustrated at myself. But I know that God meets us in our imperfection. We are not asked to be perfect—we *are* asked to learn.

And we learn a little at a time. I learned once again that the parable of the Good Samaritan is timeless. That is, it applies to us today. Just as in Jesus' time, it still breaks God's heart to watch His people pass on the other side of the road when a hurting individual is placed in their path.

I learned that God is not bound by my schedules. He is free to interrupt at any time He chooses. And I need to be ready for that interruption—for I may not get another opportunity when it's convenient for me.

And I learned that my heart bears witness to the heart of God. Had I listened to my heart's first response—my conscience's declaration—I would not have hesitated, but scooped up that sleeping boy and carried him off to the hotel for a good night's sleep, a warm bath and a hearty meal. No, it wouldn't have made a difference the next day, he would have still been on the street after we left, but it *could have* made a difference for all eternity. Perhaps that was the night he would have been ready to meet the Savior.

I just don't know what God had planned for that little boy that night. But I do know that He plans for me to be ready the next time He chooses to interrupt—the next time my conscience speaks, the next time my heart bears witness to the incredible compassion of our Lord.

My conscience and the Spirit of God also bore witness that night that this little boy was incredibly precious to the heart of God. For just as He created us, so He plans to save us.

One life at a time.

♦ ♦ ♦

He Spoke with Only a Smile

He was like a wild animal. Deserted parks, abandoned buildings, and lonely streets were his haunts. He was always alone. He never played with other children; he ran away when anyone got too close.

But 12-year-old boys wandering the streets of Phnom Penh alone were not unusual—they were among the living legacy of the mindless genocide of Pol Pot and the Khmer Rouge. Most had seen their parents brutally butchered. Conservative estimates placed the executions in excess of one million people. For most, their only crime was having an education or a career.

Despite his wild ways, the boy seemed drawn to World Vision's Pediatric Hospital—the only hospital for children in the entire country of Cambodia. Workers took an interest in the boy and decided to try to talk to him.

The task was not an easy one. The boy was cautious as a rabbit, alert as a fox. He would disappear for days at a time.

One day a relief worker got close enough to the boy to see that, under his filthy and tattered shirt, the boy carried a plastic bag. And in that bag were his intestines.

The owner of a street stall nearby the hospital had often seen the boy and had compassion on him. He agreed to help the hospital staff catch the wild boy.

Sadly, such bizarre medical cases are not unusual for the hospital. A typical day sees the staff treating over 200 children, many with horrible diseases or disfigurements. The facility and equipment would make a small American community proud. But unlike an American hospital, payment is never requested. Patients and their families are universally poor.

Situated on seven acres of real estate donated by the government across the street from the National University, the hospital's very existence is something of a miracle. Only a short time before they donated the land to the Christian organization, the previous regime had thrown pastors and priests into jail.

The hospital was built in the early 1970s. The last of the hospital's equipment arrived in April 1975, along with the medical and professional staff—the same week the country fell to the Khmer Rouge. Before a single patient was admitted, the hospital had to be abandoned before the advancing wave of terror that was Pol Pot's armies.

A building created to save lives became a center of torture. Operating rooms became amphitheaters of pain, recovery rooms became mere stopovers in a nightmarish journey of interrogation and fiendish torture. For four and a half years, no "patient" ever left the building alive.

Our confidence that God had opened the door of compassion to heal the sick children of Cambodia was sorely tested.

For me, one of the ultimate horrors of it all was the Khmer Rouge's pattern of documenting their wickedness. From 1975 to 1979, when the Vietnamese army drove Pol Pot out, thousands of photographs were dispassionately taken of the victims in the very throes of death. To this day, the gallery of the lost in a local prison is visited by family members searching for loved ones who disappeared.

When the new regime contacted World Vision in 1979 and asked us if we wanted to reopen our hospital, we eagerly accepted the invitation. That an atheistic communist government would invite in an organization whose goals were founded on a proclamation of the Good News in itself bordered on the miraculous.

What we found turned even the most cast-iron stomach. It took three separate steam cleanings, top to bottom, before the construction workers would enter the hospital to begin the rebuilding. Nothing except the structure itself was salvageable.

Four months later, in October of 1980, the new hospital opened. The cornerstone declares, Jesus said: *"Let the children come to me."*

The hospital is filled to capacity nearly every day. Oftentimes, the hallways become ad hoc patient rooms as well with gurneys lining the walls with sick children, looking like a Los Angeles traffic jam.

Rarely does the hospital staff have the luxury of treating children who have only one disease. Malnutrition turns even common maladies into deadly killers. One of the doctors examined a five-year-old girl with measles, for example, and explained, "Since almost all of the children we see are first of all malnourished, they have a lot of complications. This girl came in at the point of death from pneumonia. Her lungs were full of fluid and infection. She had purulent conjunctivitis, profound anemia and pharyngitis, and her liver was enlarged from an overwhelming load of parasites. In this case, it was hookworm.

"Frequently, a child also will have meningitis and/or malaria. Then if they have tuberculosis on top of that, as many do, they simply die. We just can't cope with those combinations compounded by malnutrition.

"Fortunately, it looks like we're ahead of this girl's problems, but if we didn't have this hospital, and if the mother had simply taken her to one of the local dispensaries, she would have been given maybe three tetracycline tablets and a couple of aspirin to treat the pneumonia. Eventually, the other untreated diseases would have killed her."

The hospital stands as the last hope before death for thousands of children.

Two boys were brought in by the father of one of them. They were checked quickly in triage and sent to two different wards. The father said his son, Chhlonh, had been sick for five months. The boy was terribly swollen. The doctor said it could be any number of ailments.

"It could be thyroid failure, pancreatic failure, rupture of his lymph vessels, rupture of his bladder or some sort of leakage problems from his kidneys, or renal failure. Whatever else is wrong, I know he has severe kwashiorkor [protein deficiency from malnutrition].

"If this boy were at a hospital in the States, the workup alone would be massive. His initial orders would have included nearly $10,000 worth of laboratory tests. But since we're limited here, I have to go almost totally on my clinical impressions. I think he has a condition called nephrotic syndrome, in which protein seeps through a malfunctioning kidney. You would probably call it kidney failure. I don't give him more than a 50/50 chance."

The other boy, Chhlonh's father said, was an 11-year-old orphan whose name was Pros. Pros had severe kwashiorkor and bad burns on his legs. The rest of the diagnosis would have to wait until later. We had no idea how it happened. When he had arrived, he had been clutching a ragged mat and dirty pillow as if his life depended on them. They were probably the last remaining mementos of his parents and former life.

Pros was lying on his mat which had been placed on a bed. The pillow supported his head. The dark brown of Pros' mat and pillow stood in stark contrast to the pure white of the hospital sheets.

His eyes were open, but unmoving. There was no breath. No pulse. His hand was cold. The nurse confirmed that the lad was dead. Pros was finally at peace. Whatever horrors he had suffered had finally taken him to his grave.

Word comes that the wild boy had been brought in. An

examination revealed he had been operated on before, and the incision had not healed. His intestines had protruded through the hole. To this day, I have no idea how he survived the streets of Phnom Penh with an open hole in his gut. . . .

The boy would not talk. In fact, the staff quickly became convinced that he could not. The depth of his trauma must have been so great that he retreated to the only place he knew to be safe—deep inside himself.

He had lost the ability to relate to other human beings.

Who knew the monstrous acts that had caused such a retreat? And who could tell where his parents were, if he had any brothers or sisters, or what any of their fates had been? We could only imagine. And none of the possibilities were less than gruesome.

We did learn that the boy's name was Chap, pronounced *Chop*. While he waited to become healthy enough to survive the major surgery that was needed to repair his abdomen, he lived at the hospital. He would still run away frequently to nearby forests, but he seemed to sense he had found those who cared for him. Gradually, he ran off less often. But he still couldn't communicate.

The surgery went well, and it looked as if the boy might have a chance for a normal life—if he was able to come out of his shell.

The first breakthrough came when a vivacious young nurse was coaxing him to count after her in French. He started to count after her, and he was so pleased with himself that he smiled for the first time.

The next time he smiled was when a lab technician took his picture and gave it to him. He smiled all day.

One of the doctors returned from a trip to Singapore and brought back a wooden train from his own son's toy box. At first Chap wouldn't even look at it. After a long while, he gingerly reached out and touched it with his toe. It was as if he couldn't believe it was real. Was it really his?

Before long, Chap was pulling it up and down the corridors. Each timid, fearful venture into relationship with the world outside himself that met with acceptance seemed to reinforce a shaky courage to try it again.

One day Chap stood watching an infant for a long time. He was lost in reverie. Perhaps he was remembering a little brother or sister who had been taken away, maybe even slaughtered before his eyes. Such memories were common in Cambodia. He stood very still.

Gradually, he leaned over to watch the baby more closely. Long minutes passed. Chap's eyes never left the infant's face. Staff members had noticed and stood by, holding their breath. What was he about to do? What was he seeing? Were they swift enough to stop him if he decided to harm the baby?

Finally, Chap stooped down, bringing his cheek to within a hairsbreadth of the baby's face. He closed his eyes, and with infinite gentleness, kissed the sleeping newborn. Chap's face glowed in a fleeting moment of joy at reaching out.

Some of the staff cried. Chap had touched another human being of his own will. Like a tender shoot, the fragile desire to relate to others was growing again. Chap's finding the courage to reach out to a tiny baby promised a time when he could reach out to others as well.

A life that had been brutally torn apart by events beyond the boy's understanding was being rebuilt by a love beyond our own. Chap's tender kiss and silent smile spoke of a communication surpassing mere words, where the Spirit of God reached down into the broken parts of his heart and began the long process of rebuilding his life one stone—one memory—at a time.

Chap still spends whole days in the forest. His most eloquent communication is still his smile. But slowly he's regaining the ability to be a part of the human family. Our hope is that he will soon become a part of God's family as well.

If Chap can reach out to a baby, perhaps soon he will respond to the One who created that babe. I thank God for the part He allows us to play in rebuilding the nation of Cambodia through the lives of its children. As in all places, one life at a time.

This is one of those stories that can only be told by the person who was there, but the themes it touches on are universal. I believe there is a common thread that unites us all when we look upon a suffering child. There is a common pain we share when any among us lose a battle, a common growth when, in the face of great struggle, a victory is won.

Perhaps it is because I have been to so many places like the one described in this story that I see the faces of the parents, the children, the staff as they confront a pain that no human being was ever intended to brave. On those faces are written the human story—of terrible separation from a Creator whose purpose was perfect fellowship, and the lifelong struggle to ease that pain of separation. For we come into this world alone and leave it the same way. Though those there be that hold our hand in the interim, we know in our heart of hearts that the journey through that door we call death will be taken in solitude. Whether we find solace or torment on the other side will have already been determined before that door closes behind us.

This is a story, then, told by one who stood by as the door opened—and closed.

♦ ♦ ♦

One Father's Cry

Nothing could have spoken to me like the silence. Nothing moved me like the utter stillness.

I stood glued to the spot as if, by not moving, the events of the last few minutes could somehow be reversed. As if, by refusing to walk away, Chiand Mia could return.

But he was gone. The boy's eternal journey had begun and the small cold hand I held in mine grew colder by the minute—it was nothing more now than an empty shell.

The boy's father stood beside me. The racking sobs and awful shouts of anguish had subsided and his grief was now quiet. The nurses had removed the hoses and needles that had sustained Chiand's life, and now his body was unfettered by the trappings of medicine's best—but inadequate—efforts. The father gathered up his son's body to begin a long walk home.

It had simply been too late. By the time Chiand Mia had arrived here at the World Vision hospital in Dacca, Bangladesh, the fever had left very little of the spark of life to revive.

Chiand's family were refugees who lived in the Demra

104

refugee camp about ten miles outside the city. Demra was a small island on the coast. But this was not a tropical island such as you see in travel brochures. It was bare of vegetation, flat, dusty—completely exposed to the violent winds that sweep down out of the north. It reminded me of the back of some gigantic brown whale to which 35,000 people clung precariously.

Chiand's first real bed had also been his last.

"Home" for Chiand, his two sisters and parents was—I hesitate to even use the word "shack," for that implies more permanence than the few scraps of cloth and splinters of wood that was their dwelling—a tentlike affair about ten feet by six feet by four feet tall.

That's right, only the small children could ever stand up straight in the wretched hovel Chiand had called home. It held no furniture of any kind. One could sit in the dirt or stoop, all hunched over. It was as if their very home joined in some awful conspiracy to oppress, to keep down, to deny Chiand and his parents the right to stand up straight, to face tomorrow with hope and dignity.

The floor was dusty or squishy, depending on the season. When it rained, Chiand got wet. When the temperature plummeted in the winter, he shivered. When the sun raged in the midst of summer, he burned, then simply got darker as the months passed.

Here Chiand became ill. His mother tried her best to make him comfortable, tried to obtain a little extra nourishment to strengthen him. She did not know he had typhoid fever. After two weeks, she brought the delirious boy to the tiny dirt-floored hut that served as dispensary to these forgotten people.

The nurse immediately set out with the boy for the hospital in Dacca. He rallied, and hope was rekindled.

I met both Chiand and the nurse at the hospital. She stopped by every morning and evening on her way to Demra to check on him. Six days had passed since Chiand had first arrived. If he had survived this long, his chances should be improving. That afternoon, we made our usual way up dark stairways, through crowded, stifling wards and eventually reached "our boy."

But it was obvious something was wrong. Commotion buzzed around Chiand's bed. His condition had suddenly deteriorated, and the medics were making a last, desperate attempt to save his life.

A young Bengali doctor worked feverishly while nurses helped. Other patients watched the drama like an audience at a theater-in-the-round. An older man stood close by—Chiand's father.

I felt the agony of his father, watching his only son's life slip away even as the doctors tried to hold on to it. Oh, God! Is there no way to help? Can't the doctor do something? The father's agony became a palpable presence. His struggle became my struggle. Somehow I wanted to fan that flickering spark of life.

But everything possible had already been done.

The limp boy became a limp body. The doctor straightened up and shook his head. The nurses began disconnecting equipment. The lamp had gone out. The oil of life had been used up to feed a violent fever. Chiand Mia, 12 years old, was dead.

The father cried a cry that must have pierced the very walls of heaven. Had he been able to do so, Chiand's father would have blackened the sun, shook the earth . . . opened the graves.

Never before had I stood so close to a father's grief. It was awesome in its breadth, the depth of its agony. But in the end, he was impotent to close the door through which his son had so quickly slipped. Though every fiber in the father's being strained to catch hold of his son as he left, the boy was beyond his reach.

Not all fathers are so powerless. Death's victims will not forever stand beyond our grasp. Life's door shall not always open and close with such caprice.

Death is always shattering, especially when it claims the young. The trouble is that, in a country like Bangladesh, we accept suffering as part of the landscape. That is, I did until I stood by the bedside of Chiand Mia.

I was prepared for the vast suffering of the nation. I had seen the pictures. I had been to Asia many times and walked among the teeming millions in the slums and the shanties. But I was not prepared for the personal encounter with Chiand Mia in the last few moments of his life, nor for the great, wrenching sobs of his father.

In the midst of sharing another's most intimate moments of anguish, I witnessed an intense drama that taught me as nothing else could the awesome price paid for our salvation. I do not mean to diminish the personal, intimate agony of Chiand Mia's father, but the tragedy in that hospital room mirrored one played out in the very heavens themselves.

I saw a love that staggered me by allowing a precious Son to die in my place. I saw a grief that, at the moment of its inception, could have rent the heavens. And someday will.

I understand a little better now how God looks at each one of us. I grasp a little more fully the jealous love with which He guards His children and the eagerness with which He looks forward to our union in His eternal home.

For if we, in our fallen nature, can so love, how much more can the Father of Light love us? And if one, tragic, solitary life can so move a stranger in its passing, how much more can the Father of All be moved by one of His children?

And how does the God of All Creation look upon you and me in our struggles? The answer is simple—with a compassion beyond our capacity to understand or express. And the same way we pass through this world: one life at a time.

◆ ◆ ◆

War and Remembrance

His body has never been found. Today, some 22 years after his plane went down over Laos, he is still listed as "Missing In Action"—an MIA.

Jim and I were as close as any two men could be in the midst of war. We had gone through basic training together. We did so much together, from shooting skeet in the Philippines to simply talking about hopes and interests and dreams to be pursued after leaving the field.

I rotated home first. Jim was to follow eight weeks later. Two weeks before he was due to go home, he was shot down.

His name is chiseled into the black marble at The Wall on panel 23 N, line 43. The cross next to his name signifies he is still missing in action. The war has never been brought to closure. No steel box has ever been handed over to his family to be interred.

Jim's fate speaks to me of how the Vietnam War devalued people, places and nations. They said it wasn't worth winning then, and we have yet to bring it to an appropriate final ending.

Southeast Asia has become a forgotten land in the world politics of today. This is especially true for Laos. Cambodia's Khmer Rouge earned it an enduring infamy as the scene of Pol

Pot's genocide. Vietnam's name is inscribed forever on our nation's monuments and hearts. But Laos, though it endured bitter fighting and the loss of a generation's hopes to war, has disappeared from our national conscience. For all three, because we didn't know how to handle the war's ignominious end, we pretended it never existed.

But in so doing, we turned our backs on the casualties—living and dead, physical and emotional, social and personal—of the war. For though the Vietnam War was planned on the grand scale of political objectives, territorial aims, equipment requirements and logistical considerations, it was fought by men, women and children—human beings with value beyond all the jet fighters and missiles and helicopters amassed together.

We turned our backs on healing. Magnanimity was the order of the day in previous wars. But nursing a sense of wounded national pride was easier in Vietnam. There was no Marshall Plan for Indochina. Instead, we instituted a diplomatic and economic isolation that continued to create victims.

Today, a child gets crippling polio because medical attention has gotten lost in a country's fight for priorities. And on this side of the Pacific, American Vietnam veterans retreat further within themselves.

The devaluation continues from a war that—20 years later—still cries out for reconciliation. Without reconciliation, we will continue to be demeaned.

I struggle with my own need for resolution. When I heard of Jim's fate, I found myself recounting every conversation we had ever had, mentally running through the list of topics we had discussed. They were many; but to my shame, I never once told Jim about Jesus Christ.

As far as I can tell, Jim perished without Jesus. What I can say for certain is that he didn't hear about Christ from me.

I can never forget him. He was my Christian responsibility and I came up short. The irony of this is painful. Jim is lost, and will not be forgotten. Laos won, and is barely remembered.

It has been relatively easy for us to distance ourselves from the war, to leave the unresolved issues alone, to pretend that the victims of it are no more. But that has never been an option for those who lived in the midst of it as civilians.

Daily reminders of the war do not allow ignoring its personal issues. One has two options—either nurse deep, bitter resentment against its injustice and tragedy or release the very real pain and face today free from the baggage of the horrible nightmare of war. To the credit of those whose homes were the site of fighting, in not being able to forget, they *have* been able to forgive. And, painfully, all warfare contains things that require forgiveness.

I met a man in Hanoi named Louang Tan. We gathered around the twisted black hulk of a B–52 that was shot down on December 27, 1972, mere yards from his front door. The Paris Peace Talks had ruptured, and only a show of force would demonstrate our resolve to get our prisoners home. Hanoi was subjected to the most intense bombardment ever in the history of warfare. Wave after wave of B–52s rained death on the city.

Louang is now 76 and has become a quiet, reflective man. When the first bombs fell, he ran to a cave hollowed out beneath his home. He stayed there, frozen in fear, for 11 days. Not until the only noise was the howl of widows and the crackle of the thousands of fires throughout the city did he emerge.

He said, "The war created only victims. Innocent people, both American and Vietnamese. Vietnamese people are just like American people. We all suffer because of war.

"The innocent people continue to cry out. There are more than we realize."

I thought about grown men crying before The Wall, the Vietnam War Memorial in Washington, D.C. Men crying for something they could not articulate any other way— expressing the incredible sadness for innocence irreparably lost, the intensity of a deep pain that has yet to be reconciled.

"Yes," I agreed, "there are more than we realize."

There were Vietnamese children playing off to the side of

the crash site. Their young faces reflected joy, the health of happiness. They had heard the story of the B–52 many times before. They were reconciled to it and the war that had produced it. There was no animosity here. In remembering, they had also forgiven.

The innocent always seem to be the first at reconciliation.

Yet we all need forgiveness and healing—not only for ourselves to be made whole, but to enable us to reach out to others who suffer with that same pain, perhaps not in the context of war, but of lost opportunities, broken relationships, shattered hopes for tomorrow.

There is only One who can bring that healing. And only One to whom we must point those who need it. I still regret that I did not point Jim to Him. But I also need to make sure that we will not forget the place and the people where he was lost. They need to hear about the Christ as well.

Jim's early death taught me a painful lesson: the Christian life requires both words and deeds. Either one alone is not enough. True, our spoken testimony can be easily set aside if it is not validated by our lives. But our actions must be accompanied by a clear declaration of our faith to be effectual in drawing those around us to salvation.

I would be failing my Lord twice if I neglect the cries, including the physical and the spiritual, which come out of this land that time has passed by.

Louang Tan put it this way, "We experienced much pain. We must relieve the pain of the victims."

We are all victims of sin, of the warfare between light and dark. And we come for healing one at a time to the foot of the cross.

There, He took for me and for you the sorrow of this world, heaping it on Himself. By one Man's obedience, many were made righteous, but the free gift of life eternal comes one life, one heart at a time. God's purpose in sending His Son was reconciliation. And now we are made its ministers. We must not fail to bring His message to every heart that is open.

As He gives life, so too do we minister in His name: one life at a time.

Pastors' Conferences are intended to be a time of building up the leadership of the Body of Christ, of strengthening the hand of those whose lives are given to His service. But they can also be times of reaching out to those in the church, but who are not yet in the family of God.

This story dates from many years ago and was originally prepared for a radio broadcast. It was discovered in a dusty box buried in the archives—but the lessons it illustrates are timeless.

♦ ♦ ♦

To Build the Kingdom

I came across a note in my Bible recently, just a date: September 13, 1957. I wrote that date to remind myself that no work, however small and unnoticed, is trivial with God.

I was in the Philippines at a Pastors' Conference in Cebu, where a thousand pastors had gathered together, praying, singing, studying the Word of God. It was a wonderful time.

We had no "official" business to take care of, no resolutions to pass. It was just a time of workers meeting together: as Baptists, Methodists, Presbyterians, Assemblies of God and Christian and Missionary Alliance—all brothers in the Lord meeting at the feet of Christ.

As one of the services ended and I turned to leave the platform, a short little man stood beside me. He asked, "Do you remember the first time you came to the Philippines in 1947?"

"Yes," I told him. "I do."

He went on, "Do you remember a little priest who had stood outside one of your meetings in the shadows because he didn't want—he didn't dare—to be seen in an evangelical meeting? And do you remember how he sent word to you the next day and invited you to come to his cottage and talk . . . then how you prayed at the end of that long conversation?"

Yes, it all came back to me. I was startled to hear the man say, "I am that man! I have not seen you since that one time ten years ago. But because you took the time from your big meeting to visit my little cottage and pray with me, I came to know Jesus Christ by faith as my Savior. The Word of God has come alive in my heart and life.

"I've spent four of those ten years going to school, and when I finished Bible training, I began a ministry in a small congregation in this town.

"I just wanted this moment with you tonight to tell you that when you gave a few minutes of your time to a hungry man—however unlikely a prospect he seemed to be—God in His own way took the words that were spoken and the humble prayer that was prayed and used it to change my life."

While I was still thinking about his words, he turned and walked away.

The next morning at ten o'clock I was back in the pulpit, ready to preach, when someone rushed up the aisle and handed me a note. It read: "This is an urgent request for prayer. Pastor Jose Clemente has had a stroke and was found lying in the road this morning. Nobody knows when he dropped, but when we found him this morning, he was unconscious. He is dying in the hospital. Please pray."

And so I called all those thousand pastors to stand where they were to pray. Before we began our service that morning, we lifted up Pastor Jose in prayer.

As soon as the meeting was over, I rushed to the hospital. When I walked in to see the dying man, I was astonished to see my friend who had spoken to me the night before.

He had gone out of his way to teach me that it is never, never trivial when we're given the chance to minister to one soul. It's always important.

As I looked at Pastor Jose Clemente's unconscious form in that hospital bed, I thought, *How marvelous, how unknowable are the ways of God, that He let me live ten years to the very eve of this man's translation into heaven's glory to tell me once more that it's not only the big meetings, the big things, but our individual contacts that build the Kingdom of God and bring men to the feet of Jesus.*

I had a sense that this little man physically had been a great influence for the Kingdom in his community. His timidity had been translated into boldness, and I knew that many souls had been led to Jesus through his life.

How blessed I was to know that I shared in that work. Had anyone asked before that day, I would not have said that evening in a remote cottage in the Philippines was important. How wrong I would have been. For God sees things we cannot. He accomplishes great things, one life at a time.

◆ ◆ ◆

No Place to Go

Christmas gives us the opportunity to reflect on an event, virtually ignored by the "great powers" of the day, that changed history forever. It's as if God is giving us one more chance to get it all right, to truly understand what He had in mind with His unique introduction of the "Word made flesh."

For starters, I think we have overly romanticized the story of pregnant Mary and crowded Bethlehem. The fear and uncertainty along with the pain and suffering of that historic night all seem to get lost in what has become a terribly cozy manger scene, replete with clean animals, soft straw, gentle shepherds and soothing angel voices.

The reality was a scared young couple in an unfamiliar town that was packed to the gills with foreigners. The situation was hardly secure; the only comfort to be found was in each other's embrace. Joseph would have been the first to tell us that this was no ordinary, serene situation.

His wife was pregnant and he hadn't even been the first to know! It had been up to Joseph to arrange for a room. This hadn't gone well either, and as Mary went into labor, it looked like the child would be born on the street.

116

The last-minute accommodation of a stall in the barn was where vagrants, slaves and animals spent the night. It was hardly the place for a woman about to give birth to her first child. As Mary labored to deliver the baby, Joseph must have felt like an irrelevant afterthought.

Recently I met another pregnant woman in an environment that will never be overly romanticized. She is Mozambican, and upon arriving in a crowded refugee camp, also found that there was "no room in the inn." She literally had no place to go.

This was a woman on the run from a war that was not of her making, but a conflict that had the potential to destroy her and her family.

I met her in a camp for the *deslocados,* those disinherited from their lands and now displaced by the savage war raging throughout Mozambique. She already had five children, four of whom had been "farmed out" wherever help was found. Though she dearly hoped she would see her other precious children again, the turmoil in the nation at the time made that far from certain. She carried the one remaining child on her back, obviously too small for anyone except Mom. The only relevant fact about her husband was that he was gone. She was pregnant and alone, humbled by the desperate nature of a tenuous existence.

There is little to romanticize in Mozambique, one of the poorest countries in the world, with one of the largest refugee populations. And certainly this population is the fastest growing.

This woman is one of many who seemed to have exchanged dignity for dependent survival somewhere along the way.

She is a late arrival, a new addition and, without a husband, immediately one of the least important members of the camp.

There is no shelter and no one to make one for her. She is given a space, a ten-foot by ten-foot piece of ground. This is where she sleeps with her tiny child, uncovered, outdoors.

Her possessions are three small cooking pots and the clothes on her back. Most of life's supports—and all of life's comforts—have been taken away. She is cautious, scared, solemn. Life is very fragile for her right now, a fact she understands all too well.

This woman represents the vulnerability of an entire nation, of the poor of every nation. Hopes and dreams are extremely frail in the massive trauma of the moment. This country and those like it cannot solve their own problems. Within the country, there's no place for her to go to be safe. And as a vulnerable woman, carrying vulnerable life both on her back and in her womb, desperately poor, all alone and much afraid, she needs our help. Very simply, she will not survive without support—food, shelter, clothing, medical care.

But in an eternal sense, she needs a place to go as well. She needs to know the voice of the One who said, "Come unto me all ye who are heavy laden, and I will give you rest." She needs to feel the love of the One born as a refugee in Bethlehem, the One who identified with the poor and oppressed of the world. The One who offers eternal hope for those with no place to go.

I don't think we can truly relate to this Mozambican woman, identifying with her need and responding to both the physical and spiritual voids that exist in her life without first responding to the Christ of Christmas.

On the day of His birth, power was exchanged for love— a love that makes each one of us significant and highly treasured. A love that obligates us toward one another. A love that reaches out to us one life at a time. A love that will be reunited with power when Christ comes again.

On that day, He will give to each of us who trust in Him a place to go. There will finally be room at the inn. He's been preparing it for 2,000 years.

White Jade

This encounter literally birthed World Vision. Like all births, it entailed personal pain and little people. And it was rich with promise. The fulfillment of that promise we are still seeing today.

The time was 1947. The place, China. The Communists under Mao Tse-tung had begun "The War of Liberation," and Chiang Kai-shek's armies were being inexorably pushed back. It was a difficult time for evangelists in the "Middle Country," meaning the center of the world. Mao's daily advances portended ill things for the gospel of Jesus Christ.

Nonetheless, a young American evangelist by the name of Bob Pierce had preached with good success in Shanghai, Hangchow, Nanking—wherever Christian missionaries could arrange meetings. His last stop was at the University of Amoy. Hundreds of college students made decisions for Christ. Upon hearing him, a tall, lanky Dutch-Reformed missionary named Tena Hoelkeboer asked Bob to stay over and share with the 400 children who attended the school she ran nearby.

He agreed, and spent four days telling, as simply as he

knew how, the Good News of Jesus to the young schoolchil-
dren. When he felt the time was ripe, he appealed to them to
accept Christ as their Lord and Savior, then go home and
announce to their parents their new faith. Many young hearts
were gathered into the Kingdom.

The next morning as Bob prepared to leave Amoy, he
stopped by the school to say good-bye to Ms. Hoelkeboer and
thank her for the opportunity to minister to the children.

Instead of the gracious early morning reception he had
expected, an imposing woman seething with anger met him at
the front door.

In her arms was a bloody child.

The little girl was still sobbing. Her back was a lurid
pattern of red lines and purple splotches. She had obviously
been whipped and beaten. Her thin dress was soaked with
blood. Her eyes were puffy from crying, and she held on to
Tena's neck as if her life depended on it.

"My God, what happened?" Bob asked.

"White Jade did just what you asked," Tena replied. "She
went straight home and told her parents she had become a
Christian, and would worship only the One True God.

"Look what it cost her.

"Her father screamed that she had dishonored her ances-
tors, beat her and threw her out of the house."

Tena thrust the traumatized little child into Bob's arms
and asked, "Now what are you going to do about it? I have six
other children already sharing my rice bowl!"

Bob held the child awkwardly. White Jade wrapped her
arms around his neck and rested her head on his shoulder.
Every few moments, she shuddered with the residing sobs.
Hot, angry tears streamed down Tena's red face. Her lip quiv-
ered, but her jaw clenched. The pain in her eyes demanded an
answer.

Pierce was shaken to the core of his being. The enormous
social implications of the gospel began to unfold in his mind.

The incredibly vulnerable little girl in his arms was a
child of the King. And she needed to be cared for.

Tena Hoelkeboer stood, unmoving, waiting for an answer. "All I have is five dollars," he said meekly. The bold, confident evangelist-before-thousands was humbled and quieted by the needs of the precious child he held.

"That's fine," she answered. "I'll take it. Five dollars will buy enough cloth for a new dress, some rice and a new slate for school to replace the one shattered by her father. When you get home, send me five dollars every month. I'll let White Jade sleep in the kitchen with the others. I promise you I'll take care of her."

World Vision was born with that five dollars. Within a few months, a few concerned Christians had formed a tiny organization dedicated to caring for the White Jades of this world.

Every time I think about that exchange with White Jade, it still brings tears to my eyes. This poor little child had, in simple obedience to her heart's new joy, told the most important people in her life that the best thing which could have happened, did happen. She had met Jesus. And He had forgiven her of all her sins, made her a part of the family of God and given her a new nature.

But instead of sharing her joy, she found pain, rejection, abandonment. On the very first day of her new life, White Jade was made to pay in blood for her faith.

That she stood firm in her declaration, choosing to flee to the missionary instead of recant her salvation, shows the quality of her conversion. She had obviously met the Man from Galilee, with life in one hand and healing in the other by His blood.

I am awed to think how God used that little girl's pain to found an organization dedicated to relieving it. I believe God does not weigh the "good of the masses against the good of the individual." White Jade's pain—although God used it for the good of millions—was not lessened. Nor was our Savior untouched by it.

In fact, I believe it is the intensity with which He shares our every struggle, our every agony, that underlies the intimate concern He expresses for each of us. Not in the thousands, but for you. And me. And White Jade. The Psalmist speaks of His thoughts to us being beyond measuring. When we lie down at night, behold, He is there. When we rise up, behold, He greets us with the dawn, having been with us through even the darkest hours of the night.

I am awed, as well, by the courage, insight and commitment demonstrated by Tena Hoelkeboer. It took one unafraid of confronting a brother in Christ to hand him a beaten child and demand a solution. And it took tremendous courage and commitment to be a part of that solution when her life was already consumed in His service. But it took the insight of the Spirit as well, I believe, to know that the question would continue to be answered every day for the next forty years—and beyond that as God is gracious.

The lesson learned that day hinged around the question asked Christ by the lawyers after He summarized the Law as loving your neighbor as yourself: "Who is my neighbor?" Jesus' answer was the parable of the Good Samaritan. It's really quite simple. My neighbor is whoever needs me. One person needing another person—that defines the relationship. For although Christ died for the world, He died for me. Not generically. Individually.

No, I don't understand it in its fullness. But I know it's true. I have seen His love reach out time and time again. But never to a group. Always to individuals. Never to "us." Always to "me," and to "you."

I have seen His face, I have felt His tears, I have touched the stripes on His back. His name is Jesus. His name is White Jade. His name is "one of the least of these."

We can change the world in His name. Just like He did— one life at a time.

"And the King shall answer and say unto them,
Verily I say unto you,
Inasmuch as you have done unto *one* of the least of these,
my brethren,
ye have done it unto me."
Matthew 25:40
(emphasis added)

◆ ◆ ◆

Conclusion

As I mentioned in the opening, this book was originally intended as a history of World Vision's 40 years of service to the poor, the outcast, the hungry of this world. It became instead a very personal account of my journey of faith and the stretching of my compassion as God has dealt with me by His grace.

My prayer is that you will join with me in learning to see as He sees when we look upon those our neighbors who need hope.

While World Vision may be a channel or facilitator, the message of this book goes far, far beyond that. It is nothing less than a prayer that we will continue in transformation, taking on ourselves the very nature of Christ.

For He came not to be served, but to serve. He came not as a mighty Lord, though truly He had every right to. Rather, He humbled Himself. If there was a consistent theme in my spirit as I experienced the events you read about in this book, it was how intimately Christ identified with and understood the struggles and suffering of those in the midst of their pain.

His identification was not as an observer, but as a participant. Not as detached in glory, but attached in sorrow. Not as risen in victory, but weeping with agony in Gethsemane.

I have yet to meet a human condition that is not graciously provided for in the Cross. I have yet to meet a man or woman, boy or girl to whom the Spirit of God is not ready with His infinite compassion to heal their wounds and comfort their troubles.

I have often felt my own inadequacies, however. Included in the material for this book were those events that challenged most deeply my own commitment, revealed most vulnerably my own very apparent feet of clay. I share that to encourage all who read this that God works through imperfect vessels.

The witness of my own heart is that the most desperate situations are where God's grace is most abundant. To the most tragically broken is given the most generous measure of healing oil.

It is this divine economy that moves me most. Jesus did not select the easy cases to minister to. He moved not among the erudite, powerful, influential people of His day to establish His church. No—He shared with the lowly. And in so doing, He confounded the wisdom of the world.

I am reminded of the Gadarene demoniac whom Jesus healed. Was this the sort of man you would invite into your newly forming circle of believers? This man ran naked among the gravestones. He was unclean, and he routinely disfigured himself with sharp stones.

Yet Jesus saw the human spirit hidden behind the chains of his demonic possession. When He asked, "What is your name?" I believe He was asking not for the names of the demonic horde that controlled his body (for He already knew they were legion), but for the name of the man—to reach through the mass of torment and touch the heart, the mind and soul that were so captured. Jesus saw not "a demoniac," but an individual man. This was one man whose pain cannot be described, but which Jesus understood.

We also see a graphic description of the relative worth of the human spirit. Jesus sacrificed a huge herd of swine in order to recover one broken man. The townspeople did not agree with His perception of value. They said, "Get out of town!" The man's dignity and healing were not worth losing their pigs.

I'm afraid we would often agree with the townspeople. We value human transformation, but not at the cost of the local economy! The Book of Acts also portrays this conflict. When Paul had the audacity to deliver the local medium, her keepers objected to their financial loss. The idol makers in Ephesus had no objection to Christianity until it began to affect their business. Try as we do to avoid it, Christianity has always had a price attached. And sometimes that price is even expressed in currency.

More often, though, that price is exacted in breaking down the walls that separate us from one another. Jesus did not avoid the Gadarene demoniac, just as He invited the lepers, the publicans, the sinners to sit with Him at supper. And when even His own disciples attempted to prevent the little ones from communing with Him, He rebuked them as well.

I find Mark, chapter five, to be a very compact summary of the gospel. In it, we find the story of the Gadarene demoniac I have already mentioned, but two other nuggets of truth are here also. In the one, Jesus heals a woman of a longstanding disease; in the other, He raises a little girl from the dead.

When Jairus's daughter is raised from the dead, we learn that it was not her faith that was responsible for the miracle. Oftentimes Jesus said something along the lines of "According to your faith, be it unto you," or, "Your faith has made you whole." But to Jairus's daughter He said no such thing. For how could she believe? She was dead. No resources were available to her to change—not even faith.

So it is with the most desperate ones we touch. They have less than nothing. Sometimes they have lost even hope itself. When there is nothing left, how can one build? In those cases, we must be as Christ and extend everything we can until life is restored.

I cannot tell you how desperate the conditions are at emergency relief camps. The people arrive sometimes only moments away from death. Naked. Hungry. Afraid. Thirsty. Every last drop of will, or faith, or any resource whatsoever has been spent just to get to the emergency center. They have certainly met us more than halfway.

Christ did not turn away from Jairus's daughter saying she had no faith, or initiative, or desire to be whole once again. No, He took her by the hand and healed her completely. He restored her to life. She had only to receive. *Then,* to believe.

Or in our case, *then* to build anew the future that has been destroyed. Ethiopia has been the classic example in our time. The starving refugees in 1984 had not even clothes on their backs. We, along with countless others, provided for their immediate needs. But as strength returned, they, too, desired to change the relationship. Dependence is demeaning, and no people will tolerate it for very long without losing something too precious to risk.

So the Ethiopian people began to desire help of a different sort. Not handouts, but tools, agricultural assistance, literacy training, infrastructure development. The result can be seen in Ansokia today. By being sensitive to the needs of these our fellow children of the Father, they are being made whole.

But it is the other story in Mark Chapter Five that moves me the most. Jesus is literally on the way to Jairus's house— facing a tremendous challenge—when an unclean woman presses in from behind. She is not on the schedule, doesn't have an appointment—doesn't even face Him directly. She just sneaks up behind and touches His robe.

He stops. In the midst of the throng of people, He asks, "Who touched my clothes?"

The disciples respond predictably. In modern terms, they would say, "You've got to be kidding! A crowd of people presses in all around you, and you ask 'Who touched me?'" I can hear them saying among themselves, "This guy is even weirder than we thought!"

The lady is afraid. She comes trembling and falls down at Jesus' feet, telling Him the whole embarrassing story. She's had a health problem, "an issue of blood," for 12 years—and it seems it's just been healed.

Jesus could have used this encounter to illustrate any number of lessons. He could have said, "Ask me directly when you need things," or, "It was not touching my clothes that healed you, but me."

But the Lord did none of these things. He simply said, "Daughter, thy faith hath made thee whole; go in peace, and be whole of thy plague."

Jesus addresses only two people by the pronoun "son" or "daughter" in the entire New Testament. The choice of the word implies a special, close, familial relationship that depends not on the actions of the recipient for its strength, but comes simply from birthright. It speaks of value. Jesus chose to mark the special value of a woman regarded as unclean by the society in which she lived. Not only was she unclean, but she was a woman. In the male-dominated society of Jesus' day, she was less than the least. Yet Jesus gave her the priceless recognition of "daughter."

The other use is in Matthew chapter nine where the palsy-stricken man is let down through the roof. Jesus says, "Son, be of good cheer; thy sins be forgiven thee."

Jesus seems to surprise us at every turn. He called a man "son" who had palsy—who shook so badly or who was so paralyzed that he couldn't even walk. His actions said he saw value not as we do, but in the heart. And here is a treasure for the Kingdom.

His second treasure is an unclean woman who has spent all her living trying to be healed. She had run to every quack and every slick huckster in the land in the hopes of finding relief. She was not exactly the kind of follower to enhance your reputation. But Jesus called her, "Daughter."

These examples show us how Jesus sees differently than we do. His values don't agree with ours. He chooses one broken man's healing above the livelihood of an entire region in Gadarene. He calls the most despised "son" and "daughter." Through us all, He reaches out with infinite compassion to the least of this world.

Why?

Because He has shared the pain these endured. He knows our common pain and has paid the ultimate price to ease it. His love has no limits. There are no extremes to which He will not go to reach the one lost sheep who has wandered off. Whether that means a stepfather frantically digging an infant out of a premature grave, or sending a medical team across the globe to serve at a refugee camp in Mozambique, He will do anything to reach a soul that hungers for the truth.

And He does it because He sees into the depths of our hearts, where we feel our personal agony and private victories when we're all alone. He sees us not as a mass of humanity, or a group of people, or even as a family unit; but He sees us when we're all alone, as He was when He died.

He understands our awful solitude in the quiet hours of the night, for He's been there. He groans with us over our intimate fears of inadequacy. He shares in our sorrow when we fall short of the mark. The founding prayer of World Vision was, "Let my heart be broken by the things that break the heart of God."

That prayer has not changed in 40 years. The scope has expanded, the resources God has granted to ease that pain have increased, yet the individual hearts remain the same, needing first the knowledge of the Savior.

Our hearts have been stirred to believe for greater things even as we have moved from caring for one lonely, beaten child to literally millions worldwide. Yet every day there remains one more just beyond our grasp. That hurts me, for I know that the next child is precious in God's eyes.

Yet in that very sorrow we find the impetus to go on. And as we learn, change and grow, we have hope in our ongoing transformation. It is a transformation that begins in one heart and eventually can change the world.

I pray that through these stories you have seen that change is not made through great saints, mighty preachers and super-human missionaries, but simply through ordinary people like you and me who care enough to let God change them for His purposes.

And His purposes are clear: to bring the hope of eternal life to the uttermost parts of the earth. St. Francis was fond of saying, "Preach the Gospel every chance you get. Use words if necessary." We have learned that both actions and words by themselves are insufficient. We must use both. Our faith is shown by our actions. Then, once established by our actions, the door is open to proclaim it directly and with understanding.

Our biggest risk is allowing ourselves to be overcome by the magnitude of the task before us. Mother Teresa understands this well and has said, "I never take care of crowds, only of a person. If I stop to look at the crowds, I would never begin." Yet without the personal gift of ourselves, the miracle will never begin. The feeding of the 5,000 would not have taken place had not the little boy given his loaves and fishes.

My service, in itself, can feel so insignificant. But only God knows what He has planned. It may be that we serve as a catalyst for a chain of events that ultimately will change the world.

If only I will begin by caring for the one person whom God places in my path. He or she is my neighbor, whether I have realized it yet or not. That is, after all, His plan. Making a world of difference: one life at a time.

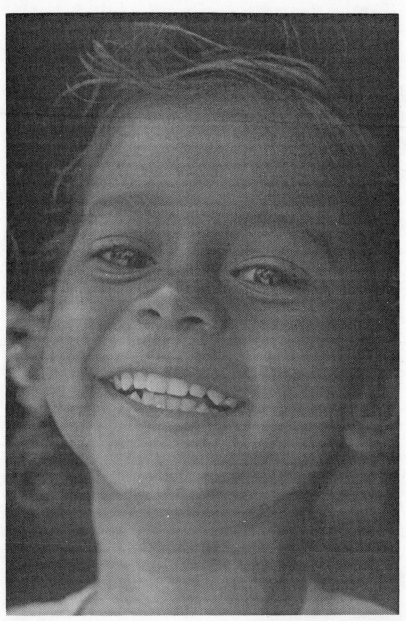

India—photo by David Ward